THE LIVERIES OF THE

PRE-GROUPING RAILWAYS

VOLUME THREE

THE NORTH OF ENGLAND AND SCOTLAND

Caledonian Railway 'Grampian' stock corridor Third No. 409 of 1906. The quality of these carriages placed the 'Caley' firmly in the top rank of British railways as far as rolling stock was concerned.

THE LIVERIES OF THE PRE-GROUPING RAILWAYS

VOLUME THREE
THE NORTH OF ENGLAND AND SCOTLAND

NIGEL J.L. DIGBY

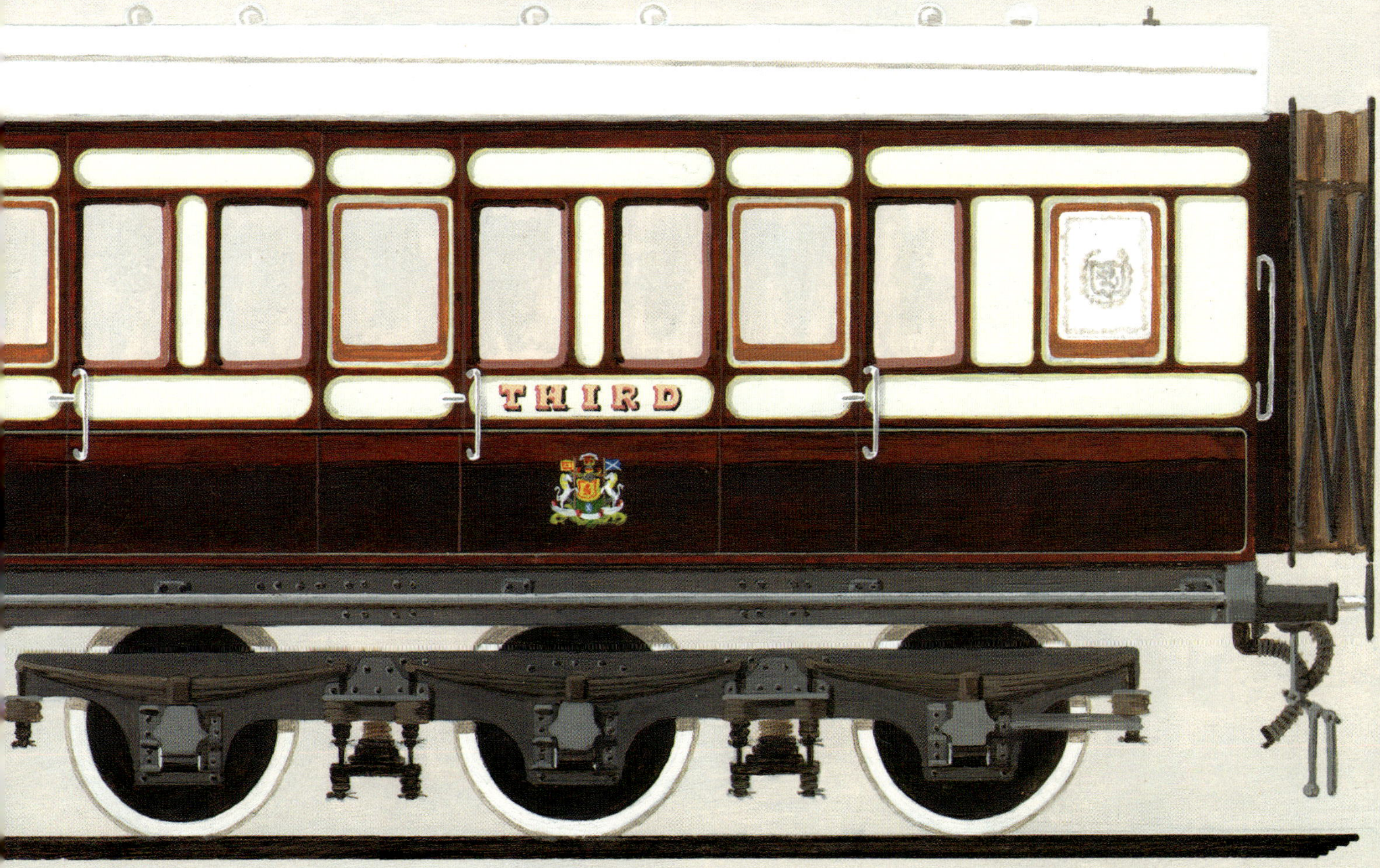

© Nigel J.L. Digby and Lightmoor Press 2019

Designed by Nigel Nicholson

British Library Cataloguing-in-Publication Data. A catalogue record for this book is available from the British Library

ISBN 9781 911038 68 9

All rights reserved. No part of this publication may be reproduced, stored in a retrieval system or transmitted in any form or by any means, electronic, mechanical, photocopying, recording or otherwise, without the written permission of the publisher

LIGHTMOOR PRESS

Unit 144B, Lydney Trading Estate, Harbour Road, Lydney, Gloucestershire GL15 4EJ

www.lightmoor.co.uk

Lightmoor Press is an imprint of Black Dwarf Lightmoor Publications Ltd

Printed in Poland; www.lfbookservices.co.uk

JOHN A. WOOD,
LIMITED,
MOUNT STREET MILLS, HARPURHEY, MANCHESTER,

MANUFACTURERS OF

Railway Carriage Laces and Cloths,

Reps, Velvets, Moquettes, Webbings, &c.

London Warehouse: 116, NEWGATE STREET, E.C.

The Manchester platform at Northwich station circa 1900, with a set of Cheshire Lines Committee carriages waiting in the Chester platform. The card was posted in December 1904.

Author's collection

Contents

Introduction to Volume Three	198
Foreword: Caledonian Blue and Photographic Emulsion	199
Caledonian Railway	201
Cheshire Lines Committee	211
Furness Railway	217
Glasgow & South Western Railway	225
Highland Railway (to 1902)	233
Highland Railway (from 1902)	241
Lancashire & Yorkshire Railway	249
London & North Western Railway	257
Maryport & Carlisle Railway	265
Midland Railway (to 1906)	273
Midland Railway (1906-22)	281
North Staffordshire Railway	287
Stratford-upon-Avon & Midland Junction Railway	297

NOTE TO READERS: Page numbers in this series run consecutively across all four volumes; Volume One is pages 1-96, Volume Two pages 97-192, Volume Three pages 193-304 and Volume Four will start on page 305

Midland Railway 4-2-2 No. 116, built at Derby in 1896.　　　Neil Parkhouse collection

Introduction to Volume Three

Volume Three in my series of articles, originally printed in *British Railway Modelling* magazine, deals with railways which were mainly in the midlands and north-west of both England and Scotland. All but one of the featured railways became part of the London Midland & Scottish Railway in 1923. The one exception is the Cheshire Lines Committee, which the LM&SR jointly owned with the London & North Eastern Railway, and remained independent until Nationalisation. Two railways which did come into the LM&SR fold but are not depicted here were the North London Railway and the London, Tilbury & Southend Railway, both of which are covered in Volume Four.

If the reader requires more detailed information than I can include in these brief summaries, then I must direct them towards the work of the Historical Model Railway Society and the livery specialists of the other railway societies, upon whom I have relied heavily. Detailed acknowledgements are given as an Appendix in Volume Four. For this volume further sketches, paintings and contemporary postcards and prints have been added. I have also revised some paintings and their text according to new information received.

Where possible, the colours are given references. The first [Carter] is from the colour chart in E.F. Carter's *Britain's Railway Liveries*. The second reference [Pantone C] is from the Pantone PMS formula guide (coated). The third [BS] is from the British Standard colour charts, of which there are several. Occasionally, where there is no close match to these charts, the European RAL standard has been employed. I have not included Munsell references as it is almost impossible to get physical access to a Munsell chart, whereas the others are readily available to order online. Rather than interrupt the flow of the text, the colour references are shown as footnotes. However, where I have good reason to believe a colour is a good match, but have no documentary evidence to prove it, I have mentioned this in the body of the text.

Nigel Digby
Cromer 2019

The M&GN light yellow-brown livery and the vermilion bufferbeam both seem very dark on this orthochromatic photograph of Class 'A' 4-4-0 No. 30. *Real Photographs*

Foreword: Caledonian Blue and Photographic Emulsion

For the preparation of this volume, I gathered together as much recent material as I could in order to revise the original articles of twenty years ago. Naturally, I availed myself of a copy of *Caledonian Railway Livery* by Jim McIntosh (Lightmoor, 2008). What I read there has prompted this discussion, which I have placed separately, rather than interfere with the text of the Caledonian Railway chapter.

The problem is what to do about Caledonian 'light' blue? There seem to be two schools of thought which are derived from two conflicting sources. The first source is from *Britain's Railway Liveries* by E.F. Carter (1952), colour patch No. 22. This shows a blue lighter than patches No. 24 and No. 25, which depict the ultramarine blue applied to both the Caledonian and the Great Eastern Railway. The lighter blue is not a great deal lighter, but still what one may call a couple of 'steps' above the ultramarine. When applied to a large object such as a locomotive, the difference would have been noticeable.

The second source is from Graeme Miller, an apprentice at St. Rollox. This was part of a process begun by British Railways (Scottish Region) in 1953. Readers of these volumes will already know that I hold little regard for the work of the British Transport Commission and officers of British Railways in the 1950s, when it comes to the painting of pre-Grouping locomotives and rolling stock. Their mistakes were many and avoidable, and are never likely to be put right. It was reported in 1957 that Mr Miller asserted that BS 2660 0-013 'Anchusa' was the 'nearest' colour to Caledonian light blue. Unfortunately, this statement is not qualified; in which way was it not quite right; too light, too dark, too green, too violet?

When the Great Northern Railway of Ireland adopted a light blue for their locomotives circa 1933, it was described as a 'brilliant

M&GN Class 'A' 4-4-0 No. 27 at Spalding in 1927. By using a panchromatic film, Henry Casserley produced the closest thing to a colour photograph of the original M&GN livery we are ever likely to get. Note the light bufferbeam, always an indicator of a panchromatic exposure. *H.C. Casserley*

azure blue', and 'bright blue' and excited much comment. E.F. Carter depicts it in his *Britain's Railway Liveries* as colour patch No. 23. Yet 'Anchusa' is lighter even than this. Had this really been the Caledonian light blue, it surely would have been given many column inches in the contemporary railway press, and even the newspapers, rather than its adoption passing virtually unnoticed as was actually the case. My contention is that 'Anchusa' (now known as BS 381C 109 'Middle Blue') is too light a colour to paint a large object such as a locomotive. If Caledonian engines had really been painted in this colour, as seen on the preserved '439' Class 0-4-4T No. 419, they would seem neither very 'Royal' nor very dignified. 'Thomas the Tank Engine' springs to mind.

So why would Mr Miller make such a potentially misleading statement? If one looks at the BS 2660 colour chart issued in 1955, one can immediately see the probable reason. There is a very poor selection of blues indeed, and I suspect that Mr Miller, no doubt under pressure to choose one, was making the best of a bad job.

Without a specification we are not even sure which blue (ultramarine or Prussian) was used in the lighter form. Royal blue, which is the name often associated with the colour since 1897, according to *The Modern Painter and Decorator* by A.S. Jennings (1921), is made 'by adding a *little* white to Prussian blue with a touch of crimson lake. Some manufacturers make a very rich blue, which they sell under the name of Royal blue' (my italics). Mr Miller's choice of 'Anchusa', being a slightly greenish blue, while in my view being too light, does actually support the possibility of Prussian blue being the base colour of the lighter blue.

So why has the notion of a very light blue had so much support? Because photographs of Caledonian engines almost invariably show them in a variety of very light greys. This, and ill-advised modern references in books and magazines to 'sky blue' conspire to create an assumption of a blue much lighter than I believe was actually the case, and when this extremely light blue is promulgated by paint manufacturers, model manufacturers, artists, and even preserved railways, one can see that it is very difficult to dislodge that assumption.

But why then should Caledonian locomotives look so pale? In the preface to *Main Line Steam*, Patrick Whitehouse described the problems associated with using photographic film or plates coated with the common 'colour blind' or 'orthochromatic' emulsions. These emulsions were extremely sensitive to blue, and insensitive to red. Skies were consistently blank white, and even the bright red of a vermilion bufferbeam looked almost black. Because of this poor colour rendering, the lightness of a light blue Caledonian locomotive is almost always exaggerated. Panchromatic emulsions giving correct colour-rendering were not popular until they were improved in the 1920s.

Unfortunately, in *Caledonian Railway Liveries*, Jim McIntosh is very dismissive of the effect of orthochromatic emulsions, going on at some length about filters and processing. However, this cannot disguise the fact that it is a real phenomenon and genuinely affects the way we see the relative colour densities in monochrome photographs. I have seen many Great Eastern Railway locomotive photographs in which even their dark blue is rendered as a mid-grey. I have also seen many engine crew appear to be wearing white; they are not, but the emulsion has rendered their blue denim clothing to appear so.

In conclusion, I cannot emphasise too strongly that in my opinion the blue was only lightened moderately, and I feel that the colour patch provided by Carter (No. 22) should be given the greatest weight when considering this issue.

Despite the uncertainty dogging the whole subject, I have taken the unusual step of not recommending any British Standard colour for the lighter blue in the colour patches, simply because there isn't one. Not even the RAL system can come to the rescue.

| 1 | 'ULTRAMARINE'
CARTER 25
PANTONE 282C
BS 381C 105
'OXFORD BLUE' | 2 | 'LIGHT BLUE'
CARTER 22
PANTONE 2955C | 3 | 'ANCHUSA'
CARTER (NONE)
PANTONE 3025C
BS 381C 109
'MIDDLE BLUE' |

Caledonian Railway

The Caledonian Railway was incorporated in October 1845. Although not the biggest Scottish railway, the 'Caley' seems to have inspired huge admiration. This may have been owing in part to its alliance with the London & North Western Railway and their shared triumph in the railway race to the North against the East Coast companies. Whatever the reason, the Caley was perceived among many as being *the* Scottish railway. The company itself certainly thought it was, calling itself 'The True Line' and adorning its locomotives and carriages with the Royal Arms of Scotland, although without any permission or justification.

The original line opened from Carlisle, through Carstairs, to Edinburgh, Glasgow and Stirling in February 1848, and by absorption of other lines the Caley reached as far as Aberdeen in the north-east of Scotland and Oban in the west, encompassing a total route of 864 miles. Its orbit was further extended by 159½ miles of joint lines.

The Caledonian Railway became a constituent of the London Midland & Scottish Railway in 1923, and passed into the Scottish Region of British Railways in 1948.

The Caledonian had its own works, originally at Greenock but at St. Rollox from 1859. The former Scottish Central Railway works at Perth were retained as repair shops. Locomotive Superintendents during the period under consideration included Dugald Drummond (1882-90), Hugh Smellie (1890-91), John Lambie (1891-95), John F. McIntosh (1895-1914) and William Pickersgill (1914-23). To avoid discussion of the early Caledonian liveries, I have limited this chapter to coverage of the period after 1895, with references to the earlier periods only where necessary.

The painting specification for Caledonian passenger and 'passenger goods' locomotives was ultramarine [1], a transparent dark blue pigment. The Caledonian locomotives in this period therefore had more in common with those of the Great Eastern Railway than is generally supposed. Passenger goods engines were those fitted with the Westinghouse continuous brake.

A specification of 1871 requires, after the usual surface preparation, one coat of lead colour, one coat of 'common blue' and two coats of ultramarine, followed by two coats of varnish. The common blue fulfilled the function of giving a coloured ground for the transparent ultramarine. The word 'common' (according to *The Modern Painter and Decorator* by A.S. Jennings) was apparently often used when estimating paint jobs in the industry, and seems to refer to non-specific and probably cheaper types of pigment. However, I believe that it must be significant that a Caledonian Railway specification of 1922 (issued to the North British Locomotive Company) uses the term 'Chinese blue' to fulfil the same function beneath the ultramarine, and this can be pinpointed as a high-grade Prussian blue. Considering the 1922 specification further, the second coat of ultramarine was to be 'varnish colour', in other words an enamel, followed by lining and then three coats of varnish.

Goods locomotive black livery on '652' Class 0-6-0 No. 664, from the Railway Magazine (May 1909).
Author's collection

202
Caledonian Railway

The ultramarine blue livery on '49' Class 4-6-0 No. 50, from the *Railway Magazine* (August 1903). At this date, the numberplate has a vermilion background.
Author's collection

Dark blue was applied to all the engine above the platform (footplate), including the tops of splashers, tops of side tanks, and the portion of the main frames above the platform and behind the smokebox. The exceptions were the platform itself, the smokebox and chimney, the cab roof, the front and top of tenders and the safety valve casing, which were all black. Black was also applied to the main frames below the platform, the brake gear, tender wheels, and all axles except the crank axle. The front edge of the smokebox and the side edges of the wing plates were usually free of black paint and burnished. The regularity and precision of this decoration suggests that it was actually official policy applied in the paint shop.

Lining was a 1⅜-inch black band about two inches from the edge of the panels, fine-lined on each side by a ³⁄₁₆-inch white line. This was applied to boiler bands, cab sides, tank and bunker sides, splashers, sand boxes, tender sides and rear, tender handrail plates and cab doors. Cab fronts also had a panel of lining, usually cut through by the cab spectacles. The splasher tops of some classes were also lined.

Edging in black with white fine-lining was applied to the blue portion of the main frames above the platform, to the small splashers accommodating the coupling rods if present, and to the top and bottom edges of the tender coal flares, forming a single panel around the sides and back.

Below the platform, the locomotive wheels were dark blue, specified in 1922 as two coats of lead colour, one coat of Chinese blue, one coat of ultramarine and one coat of ultramarine in varnish. Black was applied to the tyres and the axle ends. In the Lambie period the wheels remained unlined, but under Mr McIntosh, from about 1897, white fine-lining was applied between the black and the blue, with additional black edging to the wheel centres, also lined in white, the whole finished by one coat of varnish.

The dark blue was complemented by dark red valances, outside cylinders, tender frames and bogies, bufferbeams and step brackets [2], called variously 'chocolate', 'claret' or 'crimson lake'. It was specified (in 1922) as being, after the usual surface preparation, one coat of lead colour, one coat of brown paint, one coat of crimson lake, and finally one coat of crimson lake in varnish. After lining, it was to be finished with two coats of varnish. The use of the term 'brown paint' is unhelpful, encompassing as it does any number of the earth pigments or iron oxides, but nevertheless is typical as the undercoat of a transparent crimson pigment. The 'crimson lake' would almost inevitably have been the standard alizarin. The result would be a dark crimson, not unlike that used by the Midland Railway.

Lining on the dark red consisted of a black border to the lower, front and rear edges of the engine and tender valances, fine-lined white. Where step irons were integral with the valance, the edges were lined as part of the same panel, but where the steps were attached separately, they had their own lining. From about 1900, the black and white edging was taken along the top of the valance as well, just below the platform.

On the tender, frames and bogies were dark red, edged with black and white. Springs and the main body of the axleboxes were black, but with dark red spring buckles and axlebox covers. These were edged with the black and white, as were tender bogie compensating beams, where present.

The inside faces of the main frames, motion bracket and the crank axle were painted vermilion [3]. The safety valve levers and

Caledonian Railway

The light blue livery on '903' Class 4-6-0 No. 903, as interpreted by the *Railway Magazine* (September 1907). The numberplate now has a blue background. *Author's collection*

the rear face of the stiffening iron at the back of the cab roof were also vermilion. Cab interiors were generally painted buff and sometimes grained to resemble oak in the upper parts. The lower part of the cab was occupied by tool boxes and internal splashers over the wheels, and these were usually black.

Apart from a short period around 1899-1903, when some blue engines were given bufferbeams entirely painted vermilion with no central panel, in general bufferbeams of blue tender engines were dark red, edged in black and lined in white, the lining having rounded corners. Buffer casings were also dark red, with a ring of black fine-lined on each side with white about two thirds along the length towards the buffers. Both front and rear bufferbeams were distinguished with a central panel of vermilion between the buffer casings, edged in white, but only the front panel contained the initials and the engine number, for example "C.R [hook] 725". The majority of blue tank engines had bufferbeams painted plain vermilion, edged in black and white, but still lettered in the same way.

The style of the bufferbeam transfers in the 1890s was to have gold characters shaded on the left and below with white and black, and shadowed to the right and below in black. By about 1900 it seems that this lettering had been simplified to gold characters with white highlights, shadowed to the right in black.

Rear numbers of engines were not on the bufferbeam, but were on the back panels of tenders or bunkers in gold, 7⅞ inches or sometimes 5 inches over the gold, with a similar shading pattern to that of the main company lettering (see below), but usually omitting the shadow.

Lettering under Mr Drummond had been "C . R" on tenders and tanks in small 6½-inch characters, equidistantly spaced with a square full stop in the middle. All lettering was gold shaded to the left in red and white, shadowed in black. From about 1891 Mr Lambie increased the size of the lettering to 10½ inches, and started placing the company device on driving wheel splashers of blue engines where there was enough space.

The armorial device was a complete, unlicensed, copy of the Royal Arms of Scotland, even to the unicorns supporting the shield, supplemented by a ribbon below carrying "CALEDONIAN RAILWAY COMPANY".

By 1897 Mr McIntosh was applying the device between the letters on tanks and tenders "C [device] R", as well as on driving wheel splashers that were large enough and did not have a name on them. When bogie tenders appeared on both 4-4-0s and 4-6-0s, decorative scrollwork was applied on each side of the device. The only class with 6-wheeled tenders to receive the scrolls in the McIntosh period were the '908' Class 4-6-0s. The two '49' Class 4-6-0s of 1903 were given exceptionally large lettering, 15 inches high over the gold, and had the device surrounded by a garland based on a thistle and its foliage, but they were the only examples of this. These engines also had black tops to the coupling rod splashers.

Eleven Caledonian Railway locomotives were named. The names were curved in an arc on the driving wheel splasher, about 4 inches high in the same face and shading as the main lettering. Exceptions were '49' Class 4-6-0 No. 50 *Sir James Thompson*, which had proportionally smaller characters in order to fit the longer name into the available space, and '903' Class 4-6-0s No. 903 *Cardean* and No. 909 *Sir James King*, which used the same extravagantly seriffed style as the 'Grampian' carriages.

204
Caledonian Railway

Above: Standard front bufferbeam for blue locomotives.

Main picture: McIntosh 'Dunalistair II' Class 4-4-0 No. 772 depicted in the Caledonian light blue.

205
Caledonian Railway

Numberplates were elliptical brass. In Mr Drummond's time, they were 11 x 17½ inches, having sunken black letters with "CALEDONIAN" over and "RAILWAY" under the central number in plain block characters, and a thin black line just within the edge. Mr McIntosh introduced a new type of plate by April 1897, known today as the 'garter style', which was 11½ x 18 inches and featured two raised lips around the ellipse to delineate a border containing the same wording. By October 1897, McIntosh had introduced his final design which was used by St. Rollox until the Grouping. This was 12 x 18½ inches, and had a raised brass border and characters incorporating "CALEDONIAN RAILWAY" over the number and "S#T# ROLLOX WORKS [date]" beneath. The backgrounds to the McIntosh plates were painted vermilion at first, but later they were painted the same colour as the engines they were mounted upon. It is believed that the date of the change was 1906, with '903' Class 4-6-0 *Cardean* possibly being the first example.

Until the introduction of the final design, the builder of the locomotive was denoted by a separate small brass builder's plate. Outside contractors continued to supply engines using the Drummond design, although two later classes did have the garter style.

The Caledonian had several classes of tank engine and tender goods engine. Those not fitted with the Westinghouse brake (and therefore considered 'passenger' or 'passenger goods') were painted drop black. Several classes of tank engines fitted with condensing gear for the Glasgow low-level lines opened in 1894-6 were also finished in black, some of them having been blue originally.

There were some exceptions, such as the '600' Class 0-8-0s and the '492' Class 0-8-0Ts, which (being Westinghouse fitted) could have been painted blue but were not. Both of these classes had the unusual distinction of vermilion coupling rods. A few of the shunting engines also had vermilion coupling rods, but it was not a widespread practice.

Lining on the black engines followed the same general pattern as on the blue engines, except that the colours were now vermilion and white. Where panels of lining were applied on tanks, tenders, cabs and bunkers, two lines were placed 1⅜ inches apart, the outer line being vermilion and white the inner. The edges of valances, steps and tender frames were followed by a vermilion line, placed a short distance within the edge, with the white line 1⅜ inches from it. Boiler bands were edged in white with a vermilion central line. Below the platform, wheel tyres and centres

206
Caledonian Railway

Mr Pickersgill's '72' Class 4-4-0 No. 86 as built by Armstrong Whitworth in 1921 and painted in the ultramarine livery, with a 'garter' style numberplate. Above on the loco coal road are some examples of Caledonian wagons.   *Author's collection*

were lined with white, as were tender spring buckles and axlebox fronts, although wheels had remained unlined black in the Lambie period.

The lettering style of "C [device] R" was also applied to most black engines, but the saddletanks remained lettered "C . R". Bufferbeams of black engines were simply vermilion edged in black and white, lettered "C.R [hook] number". Buffer casings were black, with a ring of vermilion and white lining about two thirds along the length towards the buffers, the vermilion being outermost.

Queen Victoria's Diamond Jubilee was celebrated in June 1897. Two locomotives of the '721' Class 4-4-0s were named – No. 723 *Victoria* and No. 724 *Jubilee* – and given a special finish in order to haul the Royal Train. They were painted in a lighter blue, with bands of lining in 'claret' (probably the valance colour), fine-lined in gold. The lighter blue paint was prepared by Docker's Paint Company of Birmingham. Later that same year, '721' Class 4-4-0 *Dunalistair* was named and finished in 'a similar style' to the original two engines.

The new '766' Class 4-4-0s were reported in the *Locomotive Magazine* as having eight examples turned out by March 1898, of which No. 772 was finished in lead colour for tests. In July it was reported that No. 772 and engines 775-780 were painted in the lighter shade that had been adopted for the earlier three engines. In August, No. 766 joined their number and was named *Dunalistair 2ND*. The remaining engines of the class were finished in the standard dark blue.

At some date not officially recorded, but apparently between 1903 and 1906, the lighter blue [4] was adopted as standard for all blue engines. The disposition of lining and lettering remained exactly the same as in the earlier period.

In order to attain a lighter blue, there is no doubt that the coverage and density of a blue pigment was extended by addition of another pigment. What these pigments were, and how much was used, is unknown. Without an official specification, the degree of lightening remains uncertain, and is the subject of hearsay and speculation. I have discussed this subject separately in the Foreword; for the purposes of this chapter, I have used the colour patch in Carter's *Britain's Railway Liveries* and not recommended a British Standard colour.

When Mr Pickersgill took office in 1914, he continued the standard livery but a few detail changes were apparent. Pickersgill-designed engines had no smokebox wingplates, and the wingplates were removed from earlier classes as locomotives went through shops. The burnished steel edging of the smokebox disappeared. Decorative scrollwork now appeared on each side of the device on the 6-wheeled tenders of Mr Pickersgill's new 4-4-0s and 4-6-0s. A strange occurrence was the issuing of painting specifications to outside locomotive builders in 1921 and 1922 that reverted to the use of ultramarine.

The carriage livery current when Mr Drummond arrived on the Caledonian from his previous post on the North British Railway was a single colour, which is believed to have been promulgated for

Caledonian Railway

Mr McIntosh's '55' Class 4-6-0 No. 54 on a Callendar and Oban branch train. The painting shows the earlier era on the Caledonian, note the dark blue and the vermilion numberplate, although the card was not posted until 1913.
Authors' collection

the rest of the company's existence. This was described variously as 'purple lake', 'crimson lake', 'brown lake', 'red-brown', 'chocolate brown', 'dark lake' and 'lake'. These are all typical responses to a colour very similar to that used by the London & North Western Railway, being the result of a transparent crimson pigment glazed over a purple brown ground. The word 'lake', although technically inaccurate, was often a shorthand reference for this type of colour in the railway press and even official railway documents. Contemporary observers positioned the Caledonian purple lake [5] somewhere between the deep violet brown of the L&NWR and the crimson brown of the NBR. The Carter colour patch and the colour chosen by British Railways in 1957, BS 2660 3-039 'Chocolate', are both therefore too brown, in my opinion, lacking the crimson of the glazing coat.

From about 1873, passenger rolling stock had been painted all-over purple lake. The return edge of the beading or fascia was lined in yellow, fine-lined vermilion. Drummond carriages had fascia on the bottom quarter panels as well as on the waist and above, so there was a considerable amount of lining. The lower edge of the shell moulding and the extreme ends of each side were lined with vermilion. The lettering style was identical with that used in the later period (see below).

Bogie carriages were introduced in 1887, at first with Drummond styling, but subsequently Mr Lambie changed the carriage designs to have more conventional panelling. From around the same time, and certainly by 1892, the upper quarter panels, upright panels and waist panels were painted white, leaving the bottom quarter panels, upper beading and ventilator louvres in purple lake. This scheme closely resembled that of the L&NWR, even to the use of a small amount of ultramarine in the white to avoid yellowing under varnish. The Caledonian and the L&NWR were of course partners in the West Coast route to Scotland. The 4- and 6-wheeled carriages for the Glasgow suburban services remained in the all-over purple brown livery, lined in yellow and vermilion.

Lining on the two-colour carriages was yellow, with a fine white line between the yellow and the purple lake, just as on the L&NWR. A fine vermilion line was run around the sides and bottom of carriage ends, which were purple lake. Underframes and bogies were black, at least latterly, and roofs were white when new. Brake ends are reported as being vermilion, and this apparently also extended to the sides of guard's duckets when in the middle of vehicles. It is not known if the ends of those particular vehicles were also vermilion.

Lettering was generally sans-serif in gold, shaded in red and white to the left, shadowed in black to the right. The usual disposition on 6-wheeled and bogie carriages was to have the initials "C . R" (always with full stop) on the left of a central point and the number on the right. Class marking of Composites was in words on the doors, but carriages of one class generally avoided undue repetition by having only two class words 'FIRST' or 'THIRD' in the waist panels instead, symmetrically positioned on the panels to each side of the initials and number. The device was placed on the bottom

208 Caledonian Railway

quarter panels; twice per side for bogie Composites and Firsts, and once centrally for 6-wheeled vehicles and bogie Thirds. A small "CR" in interlinked and very decorative gilt script letters was placed centrally on all bogie Composites and Firsts.

In 1905, new sets of 12-wheeled carriages were introduced for the 'Grampian Corridor' service from Glasgow and Edinburgh to Aberdeen. These carriages were universally known as the 'Grampian' stock, but were also used for other express services and excursions. At 65 feet for the corridor stock and 68 feet for the non-corridor stock, they were much longer than the ordinary bogie vehicles. Their length meant that the initials, class words and numbers were spaced further apart. They also had large, ornate seriffed lettering instead of the standard, and two devices per side for all classes.

The carriages of Mr Pickersgill were flush-sided, but the purple lake, white and lining was still applied as if the beading was present. The ornate gilt script central on the bottom quarter panel was replaced by a larger and more modern monogram of the interlinked letters "CRCo". The ornate characters of the 'Grampian' carriages were abandoned in 1918. Also from 1918, all carriage doors carried class words, single class vehicles as well as composites.

Horseboxes and other non-passenger-carrying vehicles were purple lake. Horseboxes and covered carriage trucks were lined in yellow, but other vehicles such as the 'Fish, Meat and Fruit' vans were unlined. Lettering was also in yellow, but seems to have had the regular shading, on the lined examples at least.

Goods wagons were painted red oxide [6]. Body strapping, wheels and all details below the solebar were black. A specification for some open wagons of 1903 states: 'body outside 1 coat lead colour, 2 coats red oxide with varnish added for the last coat. Inside 1 coat of lead colour. Underframe 3 coats red oxide with varnish added for last coat. Wheels and ironwork one coat lamp black, with a little japan added. Wheel tyres and numberplate letters white.' Japan is a black varnish. The specification for some covered wagons of the same year was similar, although the exterior had one coat of red oxide followed by varnish. The van interiors were stone colour, and roofs were white lead.

Lettering was in white, being rather small in earlier years but increasing to 12 inches by 1900, then 15 and 18 inches as standard where space permitted. The 'C' was not quite a true circle, being one inch narrower than its height. The 30-ton bogie coal wagons had very large 30-inch lettering, with the 'C' much elongated.

Tare was in small 2¾-inch block letters to the lower left of the body, for example "6 – 1 – 0", and the load was in the same size to lower right, for example "LOAD 8 TONS". Numbers were not generally painted on the body side, except apparently above the doors of mineral wagons, but were painted in 6-inch numerals on the lower fixed ends of open wagons, and the upper ends of vans.

It is believed that elliptical numberplates on the solebar were introduced by Mr Drummond. These had "CALEDONIAN" over the number and "RAILWAY" below, in white letters on black. The plate was modified in 1902 to have a surrounding lip.

209
Caledonian Railway

Bogie Corridor Third Class carriage No. 982. Unusually, the builder has finished the carriage as if it were a First or Composite, with two devices and a central monogram. Normally, a carriage of this class would simply have a central device.

Real Photographs

210 Caledonian Railway

Brake vans were in red oxide, with their ends painted vermilion. They were lettered "C R" on the upper side, with their home station painted near the bottom, or on the ducket for those types fitted with one. Central on the bottom rail was painted the guard's name. The number appeared on each end in the top sector below the roof, and on a plate on the solebar, although some earlier types had the number painted centrally on the bottom frame member. Tare was painted in small numerals on the solebar.

Wagon sheets were in the usual black-painted canvas, lettered "CALEDONIAN" on the long sides, with the number below. Each corner apparently featured a very small "C.R" and the number. The sheet was further adorned by blue lines to form a cross but, unusually, this was arranged as a right-angled cross rather than being diagonal. One line ran the full length of the sheet and the other line crossed it, bisecting both the company name and the number, as "CALED || ONIAN".

1 'Dark blue' Carter 24 Pantone 282C BS 381C 105 'Oxford Blue'	2 'Dark red' Carter 28 Pantone 188C BS 381C 540 'Crimson'	3 'Vermilion' Carter 36 Pantone 485C BS 5252 04 E 53 'Poppy Red'
4 'Light blue' Carter 22 Pantone 2955C	5 'Purple Lake' Carter 30 (approx) Pantone 497C BS 381C 449 'Light Purple Brown'	6 'Red Oxide' Carter 37 Pantone 181C BS 381C 445 'Venetian Red'

Cheshire Lines Committee

The Cheshire Lines Committee was the result of the desire of the Manchester, Sheffield & Lincolnshire Railway and the Great Northern Railway to expand into Lancashire and to the city and docks of Liverpool in competition with the already established London & North Western and Lancashire & Yorkshire Railways. The first lines were authorised in 1865. The Midland Railway expressed an interest, and was admitted to the Cheshire Lines arrangement in 1866. The CLC was incorporated as a Joint undertaking between the three railways in 1867, with its own staff, rolling stock, permanent way and signalling. The three joint partners each subscribed one third of the capital, and three Directors to the Committee of nine.

The title of the railway was slightly misleading, as most of the system was actually in Lancashire. On its publicity material, it usually called itself the "Cheshire Lines Railway". The main line was that between Manchester (Central) and Liverpool (Central), on which it ran hourly expresses, with another main line to Chester (Northgate), reached by running powers over the Manchester South Junction & Altrincham Railway (MS&LR and L&NWR joint). There was a branch to Southport (Lord Street), and a line through Stockport (Teviot Dale) avoiding Manchester, over which the joint partners gained access. The total length of line was 143 miles.

The CLC maintained its independence until Nationalisation, after 1923 becoming an L&NER and LM&SR joint line. In 1948 the CLC was allocated to the London Midland Region of British Railways.

The traffic arrangements for the CLC were unique. The railway owned its own carriages and wagons, but no locomotives. Motive power was supplied by the MS&LR for all Committee local trains and expresses, and most goods trains. Through passenger trains from the Midland Railway consisted of their own stock, usually worked by their own engines. The MR allocated five of their beautiful Johnson 4-2-2s at Liverpool (Brunswick) shed for their trains, the through coaches being detached from the Manchester expresses at Cheadle Heath. These 'Johnson Singles' were ideal engines for the CLC's easily-graded main line, and the MS&LR (from 1897 the Great Central Railway) also supplied similar motive power, for example the Sacré outside-frame 2-2-2s. The six Pollitt 4-2-2s built for their London extension soon gravitated to the CLC, where they spent the major part of their working lives. The GNR had very little involvement in the working of the Cheshire Lines, except for running through carriages from King's Cross to Manchester and Liverpool, and possessing a very large goods depot on Deansgate, near Manchester Central station.

From the start, the MS&LR was largely responsible for CLC rolling stock, and naturally the designs of carriages and wagons usually followed those of Gorton Works, even if the vehicles were built by outside contractors. Carriages were ordered over the years from Ashbury Railway Carriage & Iron Co., Lancaster Railway Carriage & Wagon Company, Metropolitan Railway Carriage & Wagon Co., Craven Brothers and Gloucester Carriage & Wagon Company. The latter two seemed to handle most of the work from about 1900, although Derby (Midland Railway) and Doncaster (Great Northern Railway) did help with construction between the years 1908 and 1911.

Great Central Railway 4-2-2 No. 969, at Southport (Lord Street), representing the typical motive power of the Cheshire Lines. This Pollitt-designed locomotive was built at Gorton Works in August 1900 and withdrawn twenty-four years later.
Author's collection

Cheshire Lines Committee

Cheshire Lines carriages were built of teak on American oak and teak framing. A specification of 1904 is typical of the Committee's painting policy. The bodies received two coats of gold size as a key for the varnish, then three coats of hard-drying varnish. Two more coats of gold size followed, then rubbing down and another coat of hard-drying varnish before two coats of finishing varnish.

The solebars and headstocks were to receive two coats of lead grey, followed by two coats of green and a coat of varnish. Outsides of bogies and their springs were to be treated the same way. Bolt heads, footstep brackets, buffer casings and all other underframe details were to be finished in black. Solebars and ends of headstocks were lined in yellow. All of this was then 'bronzed', an application of bronze powder in shellac varnish, followed by three coats of finishing varnish. Experiments suggest that the result was similar to a metallic version of BS4800 10 C 39 'Seaweed', Pantone 4485C. Roofs were painted white, as were wheel tyres when new.

Lining was in gold on the fascia (beading). The style and amount of lining changed over time. The earlier carriages were to the designs of Mr Thomas Parker of the MS&LR, which had unconventional panelling. The top quarter panels, upright panels and the quarter lights were beaded in the conventional way, the upper corners of the windows being curved, but cut at right angles at the bottom. On the waist and lower body were applied rectangles of half-round beading. The carriages of this era, exemplified by 12-wheeled bogie Tri-Composite No. 289, built by Ashbury Railway Carriage & Iron Company in 1880, were lined on the return curve of the upper fascia, and along the centre of the lower applied beading.

Carriages for the London Extension of the MS&LR, built under the Superintendency of Mr Harry Pollitt, saw an alteration in design, where the windows and upright panels continued up to the cornice, with no top quarter panels. This design was naturally also supplied for the CLC, as shown by 12-wheeled bogie Lavatory Composite No. 234, built by Lancaster Railway Carriage & Wagon Company in 1900. The gold lining is now on the top of the fascia rather than on the return curve. Where the fascia strips are wide enough, such as around each door, the lining remains separated, but where the fascia

213 Cheshire Lines Committee

NIGEL J. L. DIGBY 2004

is narrow, as between two upright panels or between a window and the adjacent upright panel, the gold is joined into a single line. The lower applied beading is lined along its centre once more.

Mr J.G. Robinson took office as Locomotive, Carriage and Wagon Superintendent of the Great Central Railway in 1900, and it was his designs of carriage that were now supplied to the CLC. A number of bogie Thirds, Brake Thirds and Lavatory Composites were built by the Gloucester Railway Carriage and Wagon Company in 1904, all with conventional waist panels, upright panels, quarter lights and top quarter light panels.

The *Locomotive Magazine* (June 1904) mentions that the varnished natural wood of these carriages was 'heavily' lined in gold, and the photographs of the new stock do indeed show gold lining possibly up to ½ inch in width. Again, the lining was not applied to the return curve of the fascia, but on the surface, and ran along the centre of the narrowest beading strips, both upright and horizontal.

Lettering was applied to the waist panels of CLC carriages in gold 4-inch sans-serif characters, shaded in blue and shadowed in black, just as on the MS&LR. Class marking was in words on each door, with "LUGGAGE COMP^T" and "GUARD" where required.

The arrangement of the lettering, particularly of the company initials, was again subject to variation over time. There is photographic evidence that the lettering first in vogue was "CHESHIRE LINES", but when the new bogie vehicles made their appearance in the late 1870s, the company was represented by the initials "CLC" in elaborate gold script letters. Bogie vehicles carried a symmetrical arrangement of two sets of initials with the armorial device below each, and flanked by numbers in plain sans-serif numerals. Class marking was in words, "FIRST", "SECOND" or "THIRD" on the waist panel of each door. Second class was abolished in 1892.

The carriages delivered in 1900 from the Lancaster Railway Carriage & Wagon Co. used plain "C L C" in the 4-inch sans-serif characters, and there is reason to believe that this was now the standard practice. However, on these particular carriages, where a longer waist panel was available under the lavatory window, lettering reverted to "CHESHIRE LINES". An example of a

Lavatory Composite was illustrated in the *Locomotive Magazine* (May 1900) and was lettered "[THIRD] CLC [THIRD] 234 [FIRST] [FIRST] [FIRST] CHESHIRE LINES [THIRD] 234 [THIRD]". The device was used twice, placed below the left-hand number and where the name was in full.

There is no guarantee that the carriages so lettered would have remained the same after their first revarnish. Indeed, it can be shown that the new carriages built by Gloucester Carriage & Wagon Co. in 1904, which were quite elaborately lettered when delivered, reverted to a much simpler format under those circumstances. For example, Brake Third No. 265 had no fewer than three numbers in the waist, with the device placed below them rather than the initials. Its sibling vehicle No. 264 was later photographed in traffic with the standard "C L C" and the device below, flanked by two numbers as usual. Incidentally, there is good reason to suppose that 6-wheeled Thirds and brake vehicles would not have had the device at all.

When older stock was replaced by new vehicles, the old carriages were put on the duplicate list. This involved placing an "A" after the number. Generally (but not always) at the same time, after between twenty-five to thirty years running in varnished teak, these vehicles were finished in what was known as 'oak brown'. This was a painted and grained representation of varnished wood. This gave a guaranteed uniform appearance to older stock and would allow repairs to be of cheaper wood than teak. The programme of painting accelerated from 1914, so that by 1922 only CLC carriages aged ten years or less were running in varnished wood.

As mentioned above, both the Great Northern Railway and the Midland Railway were called upon to build carriages for the Cheshire Lines. The specification was for vehicles (Brake Thirds and Saloons) to be built in teak and to be 50 feet long, with a high semi-elliptical roof. However, the builders simply took the overall dimensions and superimposed their standard panelling style on them. Doncaster turned out typical Gresley GNR-style carriages, even to the lining and lettering, and Derby did likewise with their Bain Midland style.

After 1923, the London & North Eastern Railway changed the lettering to accord with their policy. The initials "C L C" became larger and seriffed in the typical L&NER manner, in gold but now shaded in red, pink and white, shadowed in black. The initials were at the extreme left of the waist, with the number at the extreme right. Class words were replaced by large class numerals on the bottom door panels, and the device was no longer applied. This was the method used up until Nationalisation.

In 1928, the L&NER on behalf of the Cheshire Lines Committee ordered four Sentinel-Cammel railcars, which were the only powered vehicles the CLC ever possessed. They were painted 'tan' or light brown above the waist, possibly 'teak colour', and dark brown below, apparently lined in yellow or gold. They were lettered "CLC" in the L&NER style.

Non-passenger stock such as horseboxes and carriage trucks were to the designs of the MS&LR or the GNR. Their finish was an umber brown paint to represent the colour of varnished teak, very probably standard 'teak colour'. Lettering was in yellow rather than gold, shaded in blue and shadowed in black.

Goods vehicles were painted a light grey. They were to MS&LR, GNR and occasionally MR designs. When new, photographs show body ironwork painted black, and white tyres, but this was probably not sustained in traffic. Below the solebar, ironwork was painted

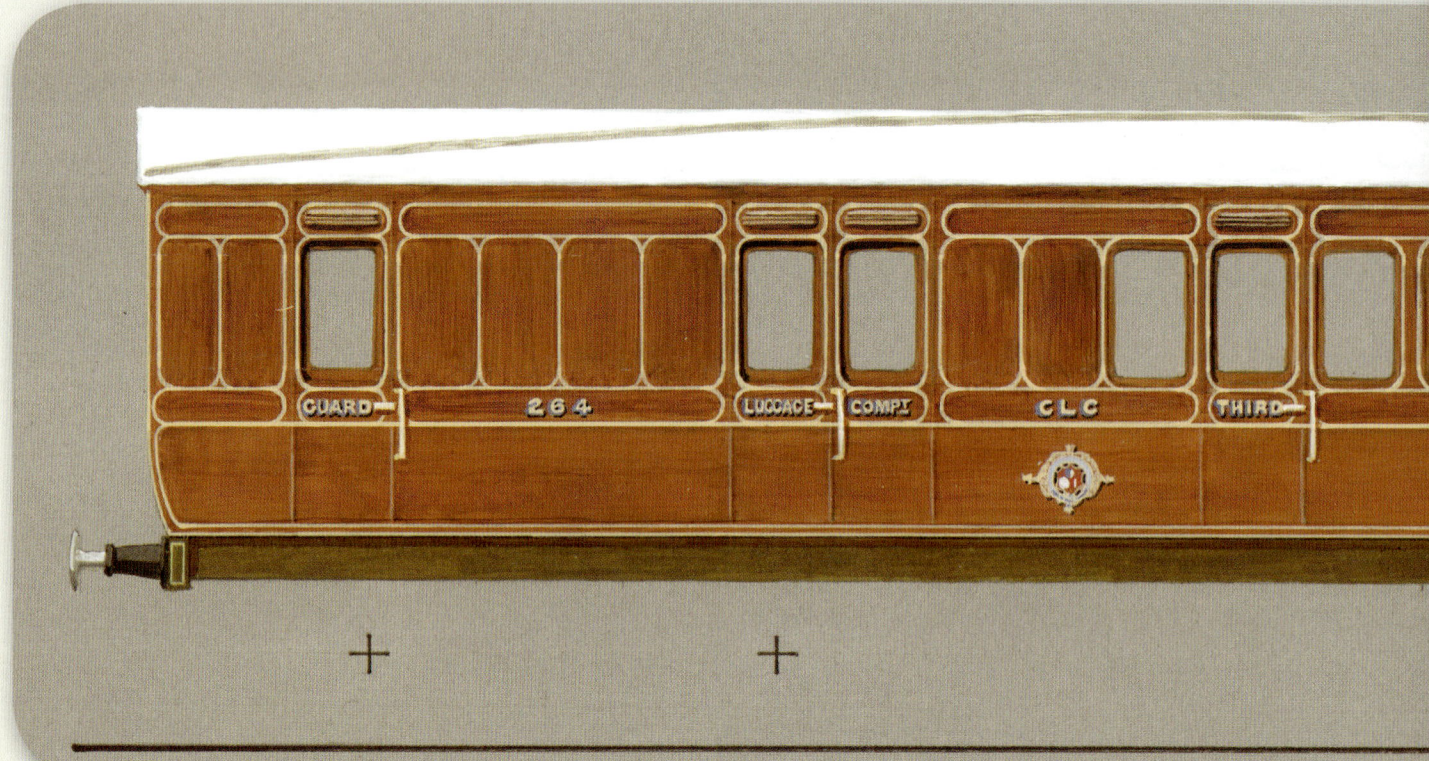

Cheshire Lines Committee bogie Brake Third No. 264, built by Gloucester Railway Carriage & Wagon Co. in 1904, as running in traffic.

215
Cheshire Lines Committee

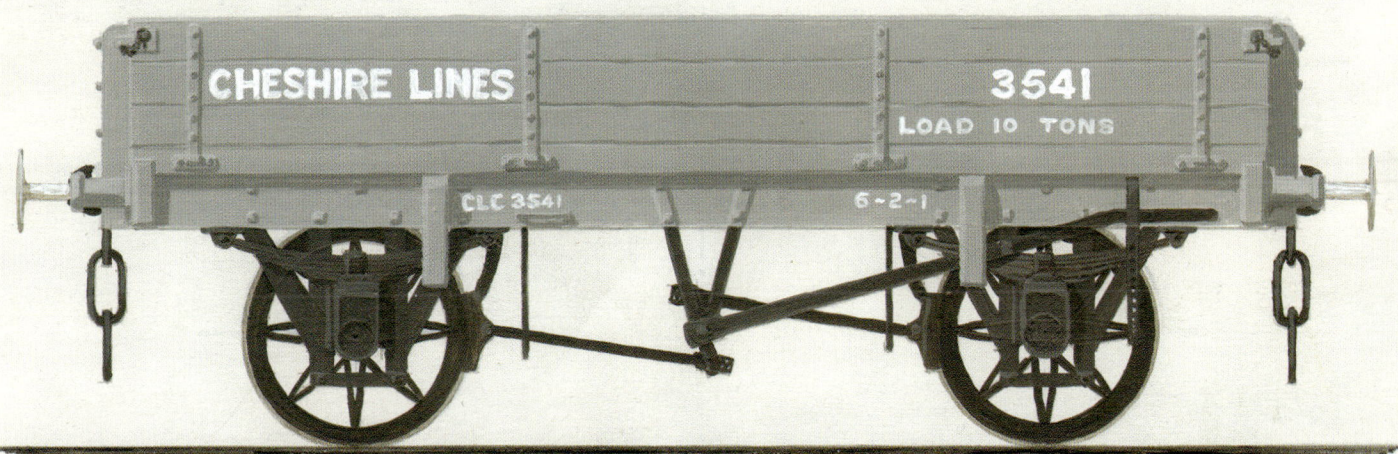

black, and roofs of vans were white. Original lettering consisted of "CHESHIRE LINES" and the number in 6-inch white characters. "CLC" and the number were painted in a smaller size on the solebar. A cattle wagon was photographed in this period with its lettering on cast iron plates with incurved corners. Higher up on the left-hand side of the central door were "CHESHIRE" and "LINES" on two plates, one below the other. On the right and in line with the name was the number "3494". On the far right was another plate "LOAD 10 TONS", with "LARGE" on yet another plate above. Using plates on wagons was a Great Central Railway habit.

From 1902, in accordance with the new Great Central style, large lettering was used. The white letters "C L" were about 21 inches high and seriffed, widely spaced on each side of the central

216 Cheshire Lines Committee

door of open wagons and vans. Some vans built by the Midland at Derby for the CLC had the initials actually on the door itself. Numbers were no longer painted on the body (except on brake vans), but appeared on a cast plate similar to the Midland style, being rectangular with incurved corners. The initials "C.L.C." with full stops was cast over the number. Load, for example "10 TONS", was painted in small characters on the lower right of the wagon body. Tare was painted on the solebar, for example "Tare 6.2.2", usually at the left-hand end.

Brake vans had vermilion ends, and had the initials "C L" closely spaced on the side, with the number above.

After the Grouping, Cheshire Lines wagons retained their markings, but by 1928 these had been altered to conform with the L&NER standard. The large letters "C L" were now sans-serif and often featured a narrower "C" than formerly. Numbers were painted on the body, below the "C" of open wagons, and on the sliding doors of vans. Numberplates were changed to the L&NER style, having a straight top carrying "CLC", but an elliptical bottom edge, along which the number was curved.

Wagon sheets featured "CHESHIRE LINES" with the number below, and had the border of the sheet delineated with a zig-zag white line, what is called in heraldry 'indented' or tooth-like.

High-sided goods wagon No. 3002, built by Gloucester Railway Carriage & Wagon Co. in April 1896, carrying the original wagon lettering.
Author's collection

Furness Railway

The Furness Railway Act was passed in 1844 and the first part of the railway was opened in 1846. By extension of its own lines and purchase of other local railways like the Whitehaven & Furness Junction, the FR established a main line along the coast of the Lake District. Barrow was the centre of the system, which was connected with the London & North Western Railway at each end. The Midland Railway also came within the FR sphere of influence with the 1867 opening of the Furness & Midland Joint from Carnforth. The Whitehaven, Cleator & Egremont Railway was absorbed jointly by the FR and L&NWR in 1878. Total route was 190 miles, including 73 miles of worked and joint lines. At first all this activity was fueled by the lucrative traffic in iron ore, but from the 1890s the company had to develop its passenger traffic and encourage tourism to make up for the decline in use of local ores. The Furness also had a considerable fleet of water-borne vessels, including lake steamers, sea-going steamers and dock tugs.

The Furness Railway became a constituent of the London Midland & Scottish Railway in 1923, and passed into the London Midland Region of British Railways in 1948.

The first Locomotive Superintendent was James Ramsden, who rose to become Managing Director and was knighted. During his time and that of his successor Richard Mason (1850-96), all locomotives were designed and built by outside contractors. From 1895 great changes became apparent under the management of Alfred Aslett, and Mr Mason's successor William F. Pettigrew (1896-1918) designed his own engines, although they were all still built by outside contractors. The engineering works and paint shop of the railway were at Barrow-in-Furness. Carriages and wagons were built there, and locomotives rebuilt.

As far as is known, Furness engines were always painted Indian red [1]. This pigment is derived from oxide of iron, being a dark red with a bluish shade. There is reason to believe from contemporary comments and illustrations that the Furness colour was very rich, not dissimilar from that of the Midland Railway.

In the *Railway Magazine* (January 1901), G.A. Sekon wrote: 'For many years the locomotives of the Furness Railway have been painted a rich dark crimson, a colour now familiar to most people ... because the Midland Railway has adopted it for its locomotive colour during the last sixteen or so years.' This richness may have been the result of the finishing procedure, or use of locally-sourced pigments, but no specification has yet been discovered. For this reason, I have decided to recommend below a slightly more crimson colour than colour patch No. 29 in Carter would imply.

There are two preserved Furness locomotives. The general consensus is that the 'Bury' 0-4-0 No. 3 in the National Collection was repainted by the LM&SR in a lighter colour after being damaged in the Second World War, and is not a true representation

Mr Pettigrew's Furness Railway 'K3' Class 4-4-0 No. 126 of 1901 as depicted in the Railway Magazine (May 1902). *Author's collection*

218
Furness Railway

Standard bufferbeam.

219
Furness Railway

of the Furness livery. Class 'A5' 0-4-0 No. 20 does not appear to be painted in a much better record of the Furness red – at the time of writing being too brown, in my opinion.

Lining was in black, edged with vermilion [2] fine-lining, and most panels edged in black with a vermilion line between the black and the body colour. Wheel tyres and axle ends were also black with a vermilion line between the black and the main colour. Footplates, smokeboxes, cab roofs, tender interiors, tender fronts and tops of sidetanks were black.

Originally, most of the bufferbeam, buffer casings and guard irons bolted to the front face of the beam were painted the body colour, edged with a plain black line. In the centre of the bufferbeam was a vermilion panel outlined in a rectangle of black, with a fine white line between the black and the vermilion. In this vermilion panel the engine number in brass characters was screwed on in the usual form, for example "Nº [hook] 36". The shanks of the buffer casings were lined in black and vermilion at both the outer lip and next to the base. By 1913 the bufferbeams (and probably the buffer casings as well) were uniformly vermilion, bordered with black lined on the inside with white.

Panel of standard locomotive lining.

Furness Railway

Pettigrew 'G5' Class 0-6-0T No. 57 at Moor Row shed circa 1920. This locomotive was built by the Vulcan Foundry in 1910, originally as No. 21 but renumbered 57 in 1918. It was withdrawn as LM&SR No. 11555 in 1930. *Real Photographs*

At first, the only display of ownership on locomotives was an elliptical brass plate with raised edges and serif characters on which the engine number was central, with "FURNESS" above and "RAILWAY" below on a black background. These plates were mounted on the centre line of boilers between the chimney and dome and were lined around in black and a single vermilion line. The last batch of locomotives to be constructed carrying plates in this manner were the six Sharp, Stewart 4-4-0s of 1896.

A new style of numberplate was adopted by Mr Pettigrew. An elliptical brass plate was still used, but the characters were plain and the plate itself was reportedly slightly smaller. Its new position was on cabsides of tender engines and bunkers of tank engines, still edged with lining. In addition, large gold letters "F R" appeared on tenders and tanksides, shaded in light and dark blue and shadowed in black. In combination with the new letters the device was now used on front driving wheel splashers or on tanksides.

There is reason to believe that the first engine to be lettered was 4-4-0 No. 32, photographed in 1897 with a train of the new bogie stock, itself in new livery (see below). The letters on this engine are small and appear to be seriffed, and the numberplate retains its former position, so this can be regarded as a transitional form.

The device incorporated part of the arms of Furness Abbey (a Madonna and child), surrounded by a circular border with "FURNESS RAILWAY COMPANY" above and the motto of the Cavendish family "Cavendo Tutus" below. The colour of the border on locomotives was red, but blue on carriages, and there were subtle differences in other tones on the design as well.

The carriages of the FR were originally varnished wood, the *Locomotive Magazine* reporting teak although another source states mahogany. Examples of rolling stock built for the Furness in 1866 by the Metropolitan Railway Carriage & Wagon Co. were 4-wheeled, arc-roofed and almost identical to carriages of the London & North Western Railway. On the drawings, class wording appears on the waist panels of the doors, for example "FIRST CLASS" in a seriffed typeface, or alternatively the more usual "FIRST", "SECOND" or "THIRD". The only indicator of ownership seems to have been a circular garter positioned centrally on the bottom quarter panels. The vehicle number may have been placed within the garter.

By the 1870s, the railway's own works at Barrow-in-Furness were building carriages (4- and 6-wheeled) with squared fascias (beading) to the waist and bottom quarter panels, but rounded over the windows and upright panels, rather reminiscent of Manchester Sheffield & Lincolnshire Railway carriages. By 1882 the same overall form was softened by the use of radiused corners to the beading throughout. It seems that during this period, company initials, numbers and class wording in the conventional way were introduced, but information is scanty. Lining was in gold around the beading, and lettering was in gold shaded in red brown. Older carriages are reported as being painted 'chocolate', which is very probably a reference to the standard 'teak colour' widely applied by railway paint shops.

By 1893, the railway's drawing office had adopted wholesale the carriage designs of the L&NWR. Waist panels and top quarter panels were abandoned, except on the doors, and the upright

221
Furness Railway

Contemporary Tuck's postcard of the Furness Railway 'Lake District Express'. Note the rich red of the engine, and the ultramarine and white of the carriages. *Author's collection*

Furness Railway Diagram 13 open wagon as built in 1900 by Gloucester Railway Carriage & Wagon Co. The number is painted on the top plank of each end. *Author's collection*

222 Furness Railway

panels reached from the top of the bottom quarter panels up to the cornice. The L&NWR also seemed to inspire the Furness in terms of livery as, from the introduction of the new bogie corridor stock in 1897, a distinctive two-colour livery was adopted as part of the new strategy for attracting passengers to the line. Bottom quarter panels, fascia (beading) above the waist, carriage ends and solebars were ultramarine blue [3]. Waist panels, upright panels and top quarter panels were white, broken with a small amount of ultramarine blue as was customary in paint shop procedure [4]. The many layers of varnish used would have lent a greenish aspect to the blue-tinted white, as on the L&NWR, and darkened the blue below. Ventilator bonnets were blue.

Lining was in gold around the panels, with a white fine-line between the gold and the blue of the fascias. The two lines were not contiguous, and a narrow portion of the blue body colour showed between them. The lower edge of the shell (bottom) moulding was also lined. Ventilator bonnets of the louvred variety had the bottom edge of each louvre lined in gold and white. Originally, underframes were lined out in white, but this appears to have been dropped quite quickly, leaving them unlined blue.

Lettering was in sans-serif characters in gold, arranged along the waist line of the vehicle, even though there was no conventional waist panel. To allow the characters to stand out against the white panelling, each letter was outlined with ultramarine blue. Numbers and company initials were about 4½ inches high. Class marking on the waist panels of the doors was smaller, about 2½ inches. Smoking compartments also had the word "SMOKING" under the class word, another L&NWR feature. In order to fit both words into the confined space, they were even smaller, approximately 1½ inches high. It seems that this practice continued on the Furness, even after it was abandoned by the L&NWR in 1903. The right-hand quarter-light of each smoking compartment

223
Furness Railway

already carried the word "SMOKING" in an etched cartouche, as was common on most railways. Second class was abolished by the Furness in 1897.

The general lettering layout appeared to vary according to size and type of vehicle, but it seems a symmetrical arrangement was favoured if possible. On 6-wheeled carriages and compartment sides of bogie vehicles, "F.R" and the number were paired together twice on each side, for example "F.R 145 [compartments] F.R 145". The device was placed beneath each pair, and longer carriages had three devices, the extra one being central. The corridor sides, having less panelling because of their larger windows, had the lettering spread out equidistantly. The 4-wheeled carriages seem to have had a simple "F.R" towards the left-hand end of the vehicle and the number in a corresponding position on the right.

The two steam railmotors (No. 1 and No. 2) and their trailers (No. 123 and No. 193) of 1905 had a special treatment. Upon the standard ultramarine and white livery, the driving carriages had their identity spread out almost equidistantly across the waistline, for example "No1 FURNESS RAILWAY No1" in the large 4-inch gold lettering. Below each number or word on the bottom quarter panels was a device, making four in total. The trailer was treated similarly, although being smaller the spacing was much reduced, with the number and word being treated as two groups, for example "123 FURNESS [compartments] RAILWAY 123". Below each of the groups was a device, with a third device fitted in below the rear compartment window.

Horseboxes and other non-passenger vehicles were painted blue and lined in white. Lettering was simple in yellow block characters, for example "F.R 17".

From 1915, during the First World War, carriage stock was outshopped in blue only, and the gold lining was replaced by a colour reported as yellow ochre, although I would suggest that this is

224 Furness Railway

a reference to 'gold colour' as used generally by railway paint shops. Lettering on the blue panels was now outlined with vermilion. The pre-war two-colour style was not reinstated before the Grouping in 1923.

Goods stock was light grey. At first it seems there was no body lettering, and body ironwork was painted black. The numberplate was elliptical, with outer and inner raised lines forming a border. The number appeared in the middle, with "FURNESS" in the border above, and the build date in the border below. Some plates had "FRC", a standard abbreviation of Furness Railway Company which the company used quite often on various items. From about 1899 a rectangular numberplate was used, with "F R" above and the number below. All plates were black with details picked out in white.

From the 1890s, wagons were painted with the initials "F R" in white, the size being 17½ x 13½ inches where possible, but smaller if necessary. The number was to the lower left in 6-inch numerals and was also painted in the top centre of each end in 3-inch numerals. In addition, iron ore wagons had the word "ORE" painted in the middle of the top plank. Vans had the initials placed in the upper part of the body on each side of the doors, and did not have painted body numbers.

Wagon sheets were marked with "F R C", in seriffed letters, with the sheet number but no other identifying markings.

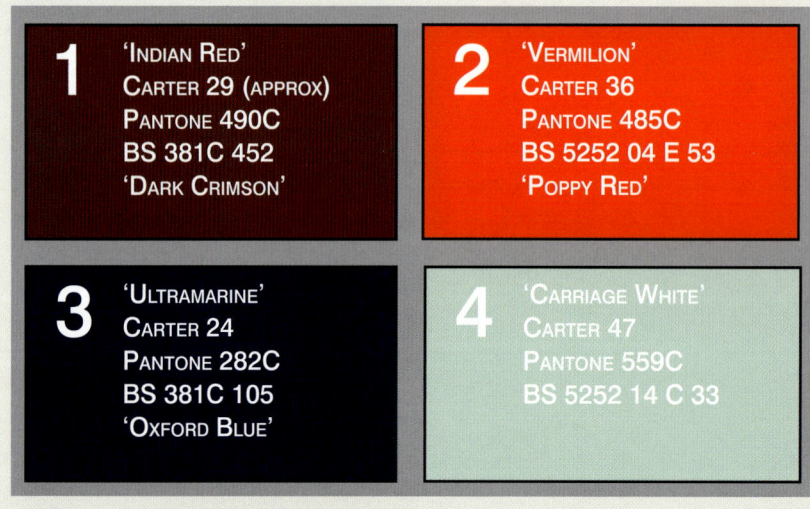

Glasgow & South Western Railway

The "Sou'West" dates from the 28th October 1850, the day on which the main line from Cumnock to Gretna Junction (near Carlisle) was opened. The new company was an amalgamation of the Glasgow, Paisley, Kilmarnock & Ayr (opened 1840) and the Glasgow, Dumfries & Carlisle railways. By construction of new lines and leasing of others, the G&SWR formed a near-monopoly in the south-western part of Scotland. It also had the distinction of incorporating the oldest passenger-carrying railway in Scotland, the Kilmarnock & Troon, opened 1812. The G&SWR owned docks at Ayr and Troon, and various steamer piers, having several steamships plying the Firth of Clyde to Arran and the coastal resorts.

The Sou'West's rival in the area was the Caledonian Railway, but their enmity did not prevent many miles of joint ownership, principally the Glasgow & Paisley Joint and the Glasgow, Barrhead & Kilmarnock Joint, and G&SWR trains ran over the Caledonian from Gretna Junction into Carlisle. The southern coast of the district was served by the Portpatrick & Wigtownshire Joint, in which the G&SWR had a part share with the Caledonian, London & North Western and Midland railways. Its main function was as a route for the English railways to the port of Stranraer. The Sou'West also worked in partnership with the Midland to provide a third route from London to Scotland, running through carriages, some of them jointly owned.

The railway's locomotive works were originally at Cook Street, Glasgow, but in 1856 moved to a purpose-built works at Kilmarnock. In 1901, the Carriage and Wagon Department was relocated to Barassie, enabling the locomotive works to be remodelled.

The Glasgow & South Western Railway became a constituent of the London Midland & Scottish Railway in 1923, and passed into the Scottish Region of British Railways in 1948.

Under Locomotive Superintendents Patrick Stirling (1853-66), his younger brother James (1866-77), and Hugh Smellie (1877-91), the locomotive colour was a dark, slightly olive, green [1], which the *Railway Magazine* likened to that of its neighbour the Maryport & Carlisle Railway. The other colour given in Carter seems to be the later Drummond green (see below). The Superintendent who oversaw the period extending into the 20th century, Mr James Manson (1891-1912), maintained the dark green, but introduced dark crimson [2] for valances, locomotive frames and tender frames (also called 'maroon', 'claret', 'red-brown' or 'chocolate').

The standard Manson livery featured dark green lined in black and white. Cab sides and tender flares were edged in black, fine-lined in white. The beading of driving wheel splashers was painted black and fine-lined in white, although some classes such as Mr Manson's '381' Class 4-6-0s had a complete band of lining on the splashers. The lining was about 2 inches wide, of black fine-lined on each side with white. A panel of lining was placed on tenders, tanks and bunkers, with incurved corners, placed about 3 inches in from the edge of the panel. Boiler bands were black, edged on each side with white.

Smokebox and chimney, platform (footplate), tender front and top, and tops of side tanks were black. Cab roofs were black, although in the earlier period they had been mostly of the Stirling 'wrap over' type, and these were all-over green. Cab interiors until circa 1903 were a dark red, but thereafter were finished in a buff colour.

Manson '8' Class 4-4-0 No. 8, completed in 1892 at Kilmarnock Works, showing the earlier Smellie lettering style applied to the new livery with dark crimson valances and frames.   *Real Photographs*

226
Glasgow & South Western Railway

Below the platform, wheels were green, with black tyres fine-lined on the inside with white, and wheel centres were edged around the perimeter with black and white. Axle ends were black, ringed around with white. Outside cylinders when they appeared were also green, lined with a standard panel of black and white, although they are often depicted as being dark red.

Main frames, valances, steps, sand boxes and tender frames were dark red. All these panels, and also tender frames and holes, were edged with black, fine-lined in white. Axleboxes and springs were black, but axlebox fronts and spring buckles were dark red, lined in black and white. After a period of time, by about 1901, main frames appear to have been painted black rather than dark red.

Bufferbeams were vermilion [3] edged with black, fine-lined white. Numbers were applied in the usual form, "Nº [hook] 104" for example, in gold characters, shaded in black. Mr Smellie moved the rear number up from the bufferbeam to the tender or bunker panel above. For the style of the characters see below.

The G&SWR did have a heraldic device (a circular garter bearing the name of the company, within which was a crown encircling the wand of Mercury, the distaff of Minerva and the trident of Neptune), but it was not featured on any of the locomotives, except as the garter.

Under Patrick Stirling, the only lettering had been the locomotive number on the cabside, and on front and rear bufferbeams, but James Stirling introduced a scheme on cabsides using the garter of the heraldic device flattened into an elliptical form, having the number within. Mr Smellie transferred this arrangement to the centre of tenders.

Locomotives to Mr Smellie's last design, the '306' Class 0-6-0s, were completed in 1893 with numbers inside garters on the tender,

Glasgow & South Western Railway

but thereafter this was replaced by Mr Manson with the lettering "G & S W R". The number was placed on the cab side, or the bunker of tank engines. The lettering was very much in the Midland Railway manner, with elegant seriffed characters. The numerals were in an unorthodox semi-serif style. The "1" had thick serifs, and the "7" had a curved tail, but many other numerals had nothing but the most vestigial of decoration. All characters were in gold, shaded in yellow-green and white, shadowed black. Engines on the duplicate list had a small "A" placed after or above the number, and did not feature company lettering.

From 1912, Mr Manson's successor Peter Drummond (1912-18) began to apply a lighter green [4]. Lining now had ordinary rounded corners and the white fine-lining was more prominent. In addition, the lettering was now shaded in red. From a specification of 1917 for a 4-4-2T that was never built, the outsides of locomotive frames were now definitely black, but the valances remained 'crimson lake', edged in black and white. Bufferbeams were vermilion, with numbers specified to be in gold leaf, the rear number being on the back of the bunker.

On Mr Drummond's death in 1918, Robert Whitelegg was appointed. Apart from renumbering the whole locomotive stock in 1919, he maintained the Drummond version of the livery. His most well-known contribution to the Sou'West was the '540' Class of six massive 4-6-4 'Baltic' tank engines of 1922, a design he brought with him from his time on the London Tilbury & Southend Railway (Volume Four). While the overall G&SWR painting scheme was followed, lining with incurved corners made a reappearance and these engines showed a departure from normal practice in having unpainted steel clothing for the boiler, dome and cylinders. The word often associated with this clothing is 'planished', but this is a

228
Glasgow & South Western Railway

Manson 4-4-0 No. 11 of 1897 was the first four-cylinder simple engine built in Great Britain. It is depicted here on a Tuck's 'Oilette' card, hauling the 'Glasgow Express' formed of Midland Railway stock.
Author's collection

Manson '8' Class 4-4-0 No. 74, built in 1894 at Kilmarnock, as presented in the Railway Magazine (October 1901).
Author's collection

229
Glasgow & South Western Railway

Whitelegg '540' Class 4-6-4T No. 545, showing the larger lettering with blue shading, and blued boiler, dome and cylinders. This class of six engines was built by the North British Locomotive Company in 1922.
Author's collection

Drummond '403' Class 2-6-0 No. 55, carrying the Drummond/Whitelegg livery of lighter green, with conventional round corners to the lining. This engine was built as No. 405 in 1915 by the North British Locomotive Company, soon renumbered 92, then 55 in 1919. One of a class of eleven nick-named 'Austrian Goods' for apocryphal reasons, this engine was scrapped as LM&SR No. 17824 in 1935.
Author's collection

230
Glasgow & South Western Railway

misnomer. Planishing refers merely to metal-shaping. These panels were actually 'blued', a rust-prevention coating which involved dipping in a hot chemical solution, giving them a metallic dark blue-black appearance.

The tankside company lettering was of a larger size, about 9 inches as opposed to the normal 6 inches, this time with blue shading. Because the builder's plate was positioned on the bunker, the engine number was also placed on the tankside above the lettering. The number did not appear on the front bufferbeam but was featured on a cast plate on the smokebox door.

The carriages of the original companies were turned out in colours chosen by the various builders, some carrying the arms of Ayr and Glasgow, but in 1847 the Board decided on a dark green, possibly the same as used for the locomotives, without arms or device. Details of lining and lettering are scanty.

Another decision by the Board in 1884 led to the G&SWR adopting a dark crimson [5] identical to that of the Midland Railway and therefore probably using alizarin crimson as the finishing coat on an iron oxide base. Lining was the same as on the MR, fascias (beading) being painted black, lined in gold with vermilion fine-lining on each side of the gold. Carriage ends were unlined crimson.

The livery notes in the *Locomotive Magazine* (March 1898) refer to solebars being 'plain dark red'. Later, and possibly from 1912 when the Midland altered their policy, solebars and headstocks were black.

Roofs were white when new, the white darkening rapidly to grey and black. In the final years of the company, a 'sandy' or buff finish was tried, but this fared no better.

Lettering appeared in the waist panels, being "G&SWR" centrally, with the number on each side in a symmetrical arrangement, all in Midland-style sans-serif gold characters, shaded in red and white, shadowed in black. Adherence to the Derby style was so close that

231 Glasgow & South Western Railway

the class markings, originally in words "FIRST", "THIRD" and so on, were replaced from 1907 by large seriffed numerals on the lower panel of each door, just as on the Midland. The words lingered on some older stock until the 1920s.

Non-passenger carriage stock – milk, meat, fish vans etc. – were 'dull red', being prepared similarly to the passenger stock but probably with the finishing coat of alizarin crimson omitted. Vehicle usage was placed on the central doors, with company initials and numbers on either side, all in 6-inch yellow lettering shaded in red. Unusually, the lettering was applied to round-ended wooden plates rather than directly onto the body.

Wagons were painted a medium to light grey. Initially, there was no lettering except for a rectangular numberplate placed in the middle of the solebar, having "G & S.W." over the number in white seriffed characters on a black background. Some wagons carried plates with the word "MINERAL" placed between the initials and the number, probably to separate ordinary merchandise from coal, iron ore and other minerals.

Mr Manson introduced "G&SW" in large white characters on wagon sides during the 1890s. Height varied according to available space, from about 6 inches to a maximum of 18 inches on unrestricted sides, as there was no particular standardisation. The ampersand always had a tail curled upward. Tare was painted in small 4-inch numerals on the left of the bottom rail, or sometimes on the solebar, for example "*6.18.1*". Below the solebar was black, and ironwork on the body was sometimes also black when new, but was probably grey in service. Roofs of vans and brake vans were white.

Service stock was painted red oxide, which bleached to a pinkish colour when old. Wagon sheets were reported in 1896 to have the initials "G & S.W" just as on the wagons (and the sheet number), but no other distinguishing markings.

232 Glasgow & South Western Railway

1	'Dark Green', Carter 16, Pantone 3537C, BS381C 226 'Mid Brunswick Green'	
2	'Claret' Carter 29 Pantone 483C BS 381C 448 'Deep Indian Red'	
3	'Vermilion' Carter 36 Pantone 485C BS 5252 04 E 53 'Poppy Red'	
4	'Drummond Green' Carter 13 Pantone 2273C RAL 6010 'Grass Green'	
5	'Crimson' Carter 28 Pantone 188C BS 381C 540 'Crimson'	

Highland Railway (to 1902)

The origins of the Highland Railway are bound up with the independent spirit of the people of Inverness, who in 1845 wished for a direct line of communication to Perth and the south, rather than the circuitous route via Aberdeen proposed by the Great North of Scotland Railway. This bold project to take the Perth & Inverness Railway over the Grampian Mountains through Druimuachder Pass was masterminded by local engineer Joseph Mitchell. It proved too bold a concept for Parliament and the Bill was rejected. The project was restarted in a more subtle way by a series of nominally independent railways. The 15½ mile Inverness & Nairn Railway was opened in 1855, followed by the Inverness & Aberdeen Junction Railway to Keith in 1858. The I&AJR worked both railways, and the two were formally amalgamated in 1861, the same year in which the Inverness & Perth Junction Railway was incorporated, the final part of the original proposal of 1845. The magnificent line over the Grampians was opened in 1863, to a junction on the Caledonian Railway near Perth.

To alleviate some of the hardship endured by Highlanders living in the far north, the system was extended northwards and westwards in stages by nominally independent companies. In June 1865 all the lines so far opened were amalgamated into the Highland Railway, the others being absorbed in 1884. Thurso and Wick were reached in 1874. The western line reached Strome Ferry in 1870. The final portion of the line to Kyle of Lochalsh, which had been authorised but abandoned for lack of money, was completed in 1897. The Highland Railway's engineering works were at Lochgorm, Inverness.

The Highland Railway became a constituent of the London Midland & Scottish Railway in 1923, and passed into the Scottish Region of British Railways in 1948.

The Locomotive Superintendent of the Inverness & Aberdeen Junction Railway was William Barclay, the nephew of Alexander Allan. Allan had been under Francis Trevithick at Crewe and was now Locomotive Superintendent of the Scottish Central Railway, absorbed into the Caledonian Railway in 1865. It is no surprise, therefore, that the locomotives ordered in this period for the I&AJR (and the SCR) were very like the 'Crewe type' of the London & North Western Railway, with outside cylinders and large outside frames at the front end, for which Allan had always claimed credit.

The livery of the I&AJR was also very reminiscent of the contemporary L&NWR. Locomotives in this period were dark green, lined in plain black. Body panels were lined out with several small rectangles having incurved corners. The first four locomotives were named on brass plates, but it seems the majority of the rest were lettered "I.& A.J.R^Y" on the driving wheel splashers in a seriffed style. Numbers were painted on the buffer beams in very large seriffed characters. Some engines carried the number on the splasher as well as lettering, presumably when the wheel diameter gave enough room, e.g. "I.& A.J.R^Y N°36". Names were carried, sometimes for a short period only, by other engines, and these also appeared on brass plates.

Mr Barclay was dismissed in 1865 and William Stroudley was appointed. It was on the Highland that the Stroudley livery, later so

Jones 'Loch' Class 4-4-0 No. 122 *Loch Moy*, built by Dübs in 1896, carrying the full Jones livery. The cleaners at many sheds used to delight in making patterns in the tallow, as seen here on the tender. This engine was withdrawn as LM&SR No. 14382 in 1940. Author's collection

234
Highland Railway (to 1902)

famous on the London Brighton & South Coast Railway, was first evolved. Both passenger and goods engines were given a two-tone livery with elaborate lining. Body colour for passenger engines was a light brown based on yellow ochre, bordered in dark olive green. Goods engines were generally in light olive green, bordered in dark olive green. Lining was black, some engines with pointed incurved corners but others with simple curves. Fine lining on the body was an outer line of vermilion and an inner line of white. Outside frames and valances were a dark crimson called 'claret'. The crimson was reportedly edged with black, fine lined with yellow on the outer edge and vermilion on the inside.

Numberplates were elliptical with a broad outer band of brass in which the company name was cast, "HIGHLAND" above and "RAILWAY" below, and a very decorative polished number centrally on at first a yellow, then a blue background. Names were transfers in gold sans-serif letters, shaded in light green, white and brown, shadowed in black.

Mr Stroudley resigned at the end of 1869 to take up his post on the LB&SCR, taking his livery ideas with him. His successor was David Jones, who had trained under John Ramsbottom at Crewe works, and had been Assistant Locomotive Superintendent of the I&AJR and the HR since 1858. Until his last designs of the 1890s – the 'Big Goods' 4-6-0s and the 'Loch' 4-4-0s – Mr Jones also followed the 'Crewe' outline for his new locomotives.

The first Jones livery, which made its appearance in 1874, is rather indefinite, save that a two-tone effect was perpetuated, complete with elaborate lining, but with the ochre superseded by a green. The *Locomotive Magazine* (October 1917) asserts that goods locomotives were painted black, lined in red and white, with vermilion bufferbeams, other sources that a dark blue-green was used, but there are no identified photographs of these engines in this period.

It was from 1884 that a more reliably recorded Jones livery was introduced, unified for both passenger and goods types. The main body colour was a light green [1], the border colour was a dark olive green, and the Stroudley fine-lining colours of white (inside) and vermilion (outside) were retained. Platforms (footplates) were black, but splasher tops were olive green.

235 Highland Railway (to 1902)

Outside frames and valancing were crimson or 'claret' [2], edged with black. There was a fine yellow line on the outer edge, and a vermilion one between the black and the crimson. Buffer beams and buffer casings were crimson, the buffer beam having a central panel of vermilion [3]. The edge of this panel was lined in black, fine-lined white and vermilion. The front lips of the buffer casings were lined in black, with yellow and vermilion fine-lining. Guard irons were vermilion.

Outside cylinders were mainly black, especially since most locomotives had the 'Crewe' design of wrapper enclosing the cylinders and smokebox, but on the body of the cylinder was a panel of the light green, edged in a black band with the standard fine-lining. Locomotives with separate outside cylinders (the 'Big Goods' Class 4-6-0s, 'Loch' Class 4-4-0s and the 'Yankee' Class 4-4-0Ts) also had this feature.

Wheels were light green with black tyres. Axle ends and balance weights were dark olive green and lined. The lining of these parts seemed to change over the years, with black sometimes flanked on both sides with yellow, and at other times yellow and vermilion.

Engine wheels had a fine white line on the spokes, forked at each end. The forked ends near the hub were filled with dark olive green. The inside faces of the frames, the axles and motion were vermilion.

There was no company lettering, except the Stroudley-type numberplates 17¼ x 11⅜ inches in size, which were retained. The background of the numberplates was now vermilion and the plate was outlined with lining. Also perpetuated were the domed Stroudley roofs, painted black in traffic, not white as often pictured. Passenger engines were named with transfers in an arc on the driving wheel splashers, or straight on tank sides in 4-inch gold block letters shaded in white and green, shadowed in black.

When Peter Drummond took over in 1896, a slightly different styling was ushered in, which remained in use until the sweeping changes of 1902 (see next chapter). The general form of the Jones livery was perpetuated, but the light green was darkened to an olive green [4], still with a darker olive green bordering. Any vermilion in the lining was replaced with white, so body panelling, edging and boiler bands were now simply black fine-lined with white. Howard

Highland Railway (to 1902)

Drummond 'Castle' Class 4-6-0 No. 140 Taymouth Castle in the Drummond (I) livery with crimson cylinders, as depicted in the Railway Magazine (February 1902).   Author's collection

Geddes and Eddie Bellas in their excellent *Highland Railway Liveries* have dubbed this the Drummond (I) livery.

Valances remained crimson. Outside cylinders were still black with a lined green panel, but in the case of the 'Castle' Class 4-6-0s this panel was apparently crimson. Main frames below the platform were black, as were guard irons. Unusually, vermilion was banished from between the frames as well, and this area was now black. Vermilion is one of the more expensive pigments, which may have been the reason for omitting it from the paint shop.

In this Drummond (I) period, the company name or initials appeared on engines for the first time. First to appear on tenders and tanks was "H . R" in 9-inch gold block letters shaded in white, light green and dark green and shadowed in black. By 1900 the words "HIGHLAND RAILWAY." had made their appearance in the same style, possibly encouraged by Drummond's introduction of the large tenders at that time. The initials were 9 inches high but the body of the lettering was in 7-inch characters and a full stop was always included. Finally, the rather bombastic "THE HIGHLAND RAILWAY." was introduced. Applications were not consistent and even members of the same class carried different versions, but goods locomotives tended to simply have the initials.

Jones 'Big Goods' Class 4-6-0 No. 112 at Inverness locomotive shed, in the Drummond (I) livery. The dark green edging is very apparent on the original print.   Real Photographs

237
Highland Railway (to 1902)

Locomotive bufferbeam in the Drummond (I) period 1896-1902.

Names were still present on the driving wheel splashers of passenger engines, following an arc sharing the same centre as the splasher and the lining. When the 'Castle' Class 4-6-0s appeared in 1900, the two words of the name were placed above the leading and the driving wheels, both curved in an arc over each, for example "CAWDOR" and "CASTLE". On the tank sides of named passenger tank engines the names were arrayed in a straight line, and company initials or words were omitted.

Numberplates were now merely a polished elliptical brass plate 18 x 11 inches, with company lettering and number cast in and filled with black wax. Bufferbeams carried "H.R [hook] number" on a vermilion rectangle lined around with black and white. Locomotives numbered 1 to 9 had their single digit number preceded by "Nº", but this was omitted on two- and three-digit numbers. Cab roofs were black as before.

The one surviving locomotive of the Highland Railway is a Jones design, 'Big Goods' 4-6-0 No. 103, built in 1894. Unfortunately, instead of being preserved in proper Jones, Drummond or Cumming livery, it has been painted in a poor imitation of the Stroudley livery. The reasons given for this scheme are singularly unconvincing. To my mind this is one of the greatest scandals of railway preservation.

Jones 6-wheeled Third class Saloon No. 53, built circa 1888, shown in the Drummond green-and-white livery. On the original print, two garters can be seen, one under the widely-spaced initials, the other under the number. Author's collection

238
Highland Railway (to 1902)

The main colour of passenger rolling stock throughout this era was dark olive green, the same dark green as used on the borders of the locomotives. All the fascias (beading) were lined around with gold or yellow. Solebars were apparently also green, and lined. Body ends and buffer casings were green, but bogies and other underframe details were black. Roofs and tyres were white when fresh out of shops.

Carriage lettering in the Jones period was a seriffed style in gold. Shading was in green and white, shadowed in black. The lettering seems to have varied with the class of vehicle. Carriages of uniform class were lettered in the waist in full. Some stock carried "FIRST/CLASS" or "THIRD/CLASS" on each side of the central door, but ordinary Thirds seem to have been marked simply as "THIRD/THIRD". Composites had the class marking on each door. By the end of the Jones period there are indications that a plain block style of characters was being introduced.

Many passenger vehicles carried a 10-inch garter in gold, with "HIGHLAND RAILWAY COMPANY" disposed around it. The garter was placed centrally on the lower body, but probably not on Thirds or Brakes. Where the garter did appear, the carriage number was placed within it, hence First class and Composites generally carried no number in the waist panels. Other carriages had "H.R" and the number in the waist. At each end of the carriage, a script monogram of the initials "HR" was placed.

From 1897 under Mr Drummond, after an experiment with the Duke of Sutherland's private Saloon, the Board decided to have the upper panels (waist panel, upright panel, top quarter panel) of all carriages painted white. The fascia (beading) and droplights remained green, and lining was still in gold or yellow.

The lettering style was changed, the monograms being abandoned, and numbers and "H . R" widely-spaced appearing in the waist of all carriages, in sans-serif gold characters, shaded in green and white

239
Highland Railway (to 1902)

and shadowed in black. Two garters were now the rule, and two numbers were placed symmetrically on the longer vehicles, usually above the garters. Class marking was still generally on the waist panels, now even extended to Composites, for example on a bogie Lavatory Composite of 1898: "[door] THIRD [door] 47 [door] THIRD [door] H . R [door] 47 [door] FIRST [door]". The garter was placed below the two numbers.

Full brake vehicles were lettered "LUGGAGE [ducket] [GUARD] VAN" on the waist panels on either side of the central ducket, and usually had the intials "H R" placed on the upright panels of the ducket, with the number in the waist panel. There were no garters. Brake ends of carriages were painted vermilion.

RIGHT: Drummond (I) carriage livery 1897-1902.

240 Highland Railway (to 1902)

Until 1896 the colour of goods vehicles was 'claret' or crimson. Below the solebar was black, although wheel tyres were white when new. The only written sign of ownership was the large elliptical numberplate, carrying "HIGHLAND RAILWAY" over the number and "TO CARRY 8 TONS" (for example) below, painted black with white lettering. Some wagons carried a symbol on the upper left, consisting of a 9-inch white ring enclosing a yellow shield carrying 'H' overlapped by a white shield carrying 'R', the letters being in the body colour.

Goods brake vans in the Jones period were 'claret', with yellow lettering shaded in vermilion, and vermilion ends. Their interiors were buff.

After 1896, goods stock was painted red oxide, which would no doubt have been a much cheaper alternative. Letters "H R" up to 12 inches high were applied to wagon sides. For some time the old symbol mentioned above was retained, with the wagon number in small numerals below, but the standard became 4-inch numerals, usually applied to the lower left, and to each end of the wagon.

Goods brakes were red oxide, although being varnished they apparently looked a richer colour. Lettering was now in white, the initials "H R" and the words "GOODS BRAKE" being in various arrangements. The number was usually on the guard's ducket.

Wagon sheets were in the usual black-painted canvas, and the main lettering along the major sides was "HIGHLAND R^{Y}" with the number below. At one end was "H . R^{Y}" with the number at the opposite end. There were no other distinguishing marks.

1 'LIGHT GREEN'
CARTER 18
PANTONE 377C
BS 5252 12 E 55

2 'CLARET'
CARTER 27
PANTONE 1817C
BS 381C 449
'LIGHT PURPLE BROWN'

3 'VERMILION'
CARTER 36
PANTONE 485C
BS 5252 04 E 53
'POPPY RED'

4 'OLIVE GREEN'
CARTER 12
PANTONE 574C
BS 381C 220
'OLIVE GREEN'

Highland Railway (from 1902)

The liveries of the Highland Railway under David Jones and the alterations instituted by his successor Peter Drummond have been recounted in the previous chapter.

By the end of 1902 the finances of the Highland Railway were such that from September of that year more economical painting styles were ordered, noticed by the railway press during 1903. A much plainer livery was adopted, essentially maintained by Mr Drummond's successors Mr F.G. Smith (1912-15), Mr C. Cumming (1915-22) and Mr D.C. Urie (1922).

The new Highland locomotive style was still based on green, but used a much darker overall olive green [1] without any bordering. All lining was abandoned, although it is believed that there may have been a short transition period when lining was still applied to the dark green. The application of this olive green Drummond (II) livery was unique in that even bufferbeams were green, probably because vermilion was one of the more expensive pigments. The usual black areas such as smokeboxes, platforms (footplates) and cab roofs remained black. Below the platform, valances and outside cylinders were green except on the older types of locomotive where the cylinders were included in the smokebox wrapper, and so were black. Locomotive and tender frames were black. Wheels were green, with black tyres.

In the Drummond (I) period, numberplates had been polished elliptical brass with company lettering and number cast and filled with black wax, and bufferbeams carried "H.R [hook] number" on a vermilion rectangle lined around with black and white. For the new Drummond (II) period, the brass numberplate was redesigned. It was increased in size to 22½ x 15⅜ inches and had two raised beadings forming a border with "HIGHLAND RAILWAY" arranged on it around the central number, all on a black background. The bufferbeam lettering remained unchanged, but now on a plain green background.

All lettering styles from 1896 to 1922 used plain sans-serif characters in gold, shaded in dark and light green to the left, highlighted in white, and shadowed in black to the right. There were at first three arrangements, applied in a rather inconsistent manner. Generally, goods engines and shunting tank engines tended to have "H . R" in widely-spaced 9-inch letters with the full stop centrally between them. Some of the passenger engines with small tenders also had this. The most common lettering for passenger engines, both

'Big Ben' Class 4-4-0 No. 61 Ben na Caillich, built in 1908, as depicted in the Railway Magazine (December 1908), showing the plain green Drummond (II) livery. The black background to the numberplate is correct but the green applied by the printer more resembles the Drummond (I) colour.
Author's collection

242
Highland Railway (from 1902)

tank and tender, was "HIGHLAND RAILWAY." including a full stop. Most of the lettering was 7 inches high, but the initials were 9 inches. A less common style was "THE HIGHLAND RAILWAY.", seen on all types of locomotive at random, for example the 0-6-4T banking engines of 1909. The engine number was applied to the rear of tenders and bunkers in 9-inch numerals. Many engines were named, and these were applied in a curve on splashers, or straight on tank sides in 4-inch characters.

Mr Smith's tenure was too short for his alterations to affect all the locomotive stock. He is said to have lightened the engine green, and illustrations tend to suggest that it reverted to something approximating the earlier Drummond (I) green. The most noticeable difference was the reintroduction of vermilion bufferbeams, now lettered simply "H [hook] R".

Brass numberplates were removed from engines coming through shops to be melted down. In their place the same transfer numerals which had been used on the rear of engines were now applied to the upper part of the cabside. Some engines also received small cut-out metal numbers on their smokebox doors. Lettering was simplified to "H · R" on all engines, the central full stop now being on the horizontal centreline of the initials. Many of these changes were applied inconsistently, resulting in a number of hybrids.

On Mr Cumming assuming command after Mr Smith's resignation in 1915 (following the 'River' Class 4-6-0 debacle), the

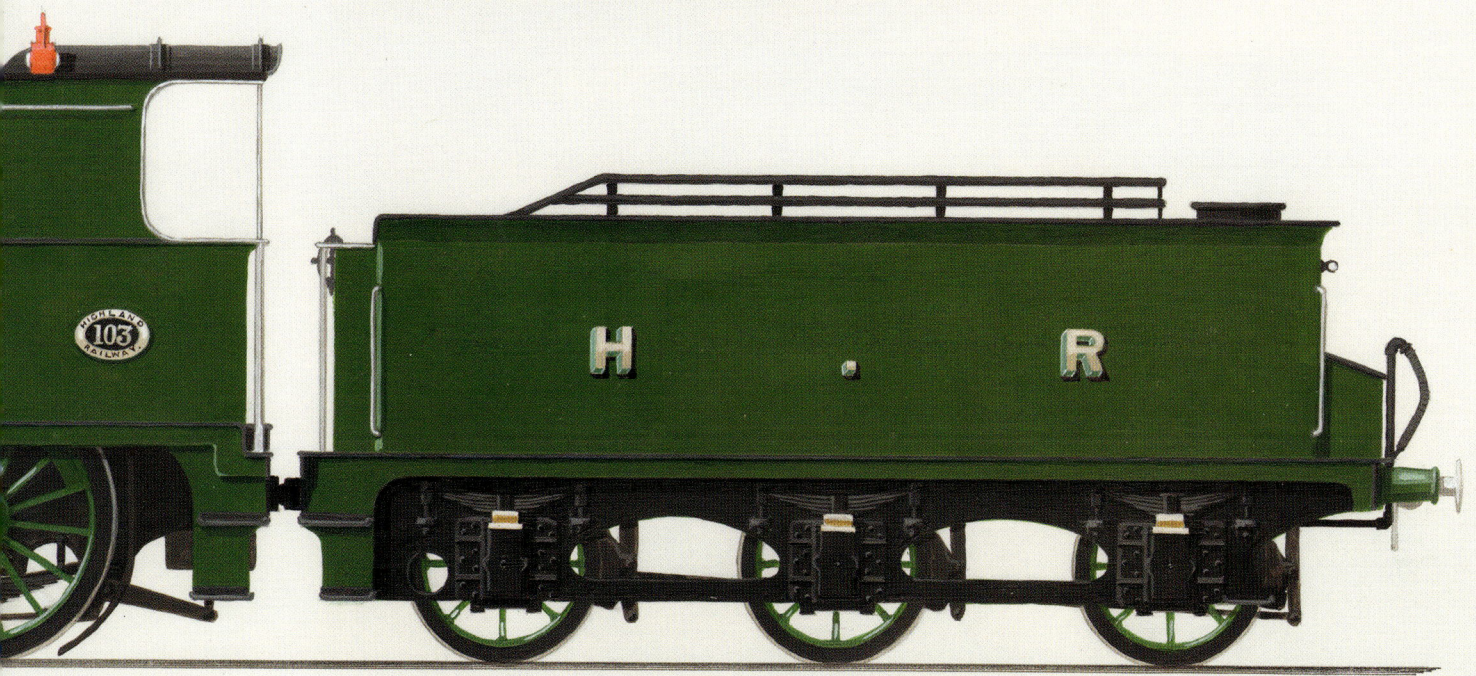

Highland Railway (from 1902)

engine green was apparently darkened slightly, but circumstances during and after the First World War meant that the colour was subject to immense variation and the locomotive fleet would not have had a uniform appearance. Some of the last engines built for the Highland, by Hawthorn, Leslie of Newcastle in 1921, were turned out in a light yellowish green, but this is an example of the rather loose interpretation of a painting specification in which engine builders often indulged. Axle ends were now black.

Lettering remained "H . R", but now 12 inches high and the full stop eventually resumed its former position on the baseline. Numberplates were reintroduced. Mr Cumming's two 'Snaigow' Class 4-4-0s had a hybrid pattern reusing the Jones design, but generally plates were to the Drummond (II) pattern, this time in gunmetal and thus had a bronze colour on the polished surfaces. Preserved Jones 'Big Goods' 4-6-0 No. 103 has a gunmetal numberplate, which suggests a more valid style of livery that could be applied!

Forward bufferbeams now carried "Nº [hook] xxx", but rear numbers remained unaltered. From 1916 the armorial device appeared on the splashers of Mr Cumming's new engines, the 'Snaigow' Class 4-4-0s, the 'Clan' Class 4-6-0s, and the 'Clan Goods' Class 4-6-0s.

From 1897, carriage livery had been dark olive green with white upper panels. From September 1902 the white upper panels were

Highland Railway (from 1902)
244

Drummond 'X' Class 0-6-4T No. 68 in the plain green Drummond (II) livery. Built as No. 65 by the North British Locomotive Co. in 1909, the engine was almost immediately renumbered. It was withdrawn as LM&SR No. 15302 in 1933.
Author's collection

Cumming 4-4-0 No. 73 *Snaigow* as shown in the *Railway & Travel Monthly* of February 1917. The two plates are incorrectly shown with vermilion backgrounds. Another painting of the same engine appeared in the *Railway Magazine*, but with correct black backgrounds to the plates. The central full-stop between the initials is still in the Smith position. *Author's collection*

245
Highland Railway (from 1902)

Cumming 'Clan' Class 4-6-0 No. 49 *Clan Campbell* in the full Cumming livery, with device and gunmetal numberplate. Note the number on the bufferbeam. Built in 1919, the locomotive was withdrawn as LM&SR No. 14762 in 1947.   *Real Photographs*

Lavatory Brake Composite No. 18 of 1911 illustrates the vertical matchboarding style, and the larger lettering that resulted.   *Author's collection*

246
Highland Railway (from 1902)

discontinued and the locomotive dark green [1] was applied without any lining. Carriages remained painted the current locomotive green until the Grouping. Solebars and bogies were black, and Mansell wheels had varnished teak centres and white tyres when freshly painted. It is suggested that carriage roofs from 1903 to 1912 were medium grey, but many photographs show white roofs as usual during this period.

The characters used in carriage lettering remained constant from 1897 to 1922, only the size varying from period to period. Letters and numbers were gold sans-serif, shaded in green and white and shadowed in black just as on the locomotives. On the conventionally-panelled carriages, class marking, numbers and initials were all in 4-inch characters in the waist panels. Initials were "H . R" applied once per side. On shorter 4- and 6-wheeled vehicles, they were placed to left of centre, with the number in a corresponding position on the right. On bogie vehicles the initials were placed as centrally as possible, with two numbers on each side arranged symmetrically. Class marking was now in the waist panel of each door. Two garters, part of the armorial device, carrying "HIGHLAND RAILWAY COMPANY" around them were placed in the lower panels of most stock except luggage brake vans.

In 1906, two special sleeping carriages and two excursion Saloons were built by outside contractors. They had a new style of using vertical matchboarding below the windows, replacing the waist and bottom quarter panels. In addition to that, they were built of teak

Highland Railway (from 1902)

and varnished. The carriages had end vestibules, the door of one end marked "THIRD" with "FIRST" at the other, in the usual lettering. Centrally was an ellipse of beading, containing "H.R/Nº 8" (for example) on two lines in much larger characters. The words "SLEEPING" and "CARRIAGE" were disposed on each side of the ellipse in these large characters, with two garters beyond. The lavatory windows were etched with a representation of the armorial garter containing the letters "HR".

From 1907 the new style of vertical matchboarding was extended to all new carriages. This freed the lettering from the constraints of the waist panels and henceforth these vehicles, and those of the older types rebuilt to resemble them, carried much larger characters placed lower on the bodies than before. Initials were now usually central and 7 inches high, with two 9-inch-high numbers disposed symmetrically at each side, although the vestibule corridor coaches of 1909 had only one set of initials and one number on each side. Class marking remained in 4-inch-high characters and was frequently not in alignment with the other lettering. The two garters on each side also remained. Mr Smith replaced them from 1912 with the full device on new stock.

Horseboxes and carriage trucks were painted the current carriage green, lettered in yellow shaded to right and below in black. In 1912 a number of fitted fish wagons which were previously painted as for goods stock were transferred to passenger stock and repainted green with plain yellow lettering. Some meat vans were also apparently transferred in this way.

248
Highland Railway (from 1902)

Goods stock from 1896 was painted red oxide [2], described as a rich red-brown, the equivalent of Indian red. Lettering was a large "H R" in white block letters, a minimum of 12 inches high on most wagons, and often 15 inches or 18 inches. Cattle and sheep wagons had smaller 9-inch initials on their top planks. Numbers were often on the lower left, but could appear elsewhere. Numbers were also applied to the ends of most vehicles in small 4-inch numerals. The Jones elliptical numberplate was still used for some time, but later the only numbers were those on the body. Wagons without plates had the load capacity painted on the lower right.

1 'Dark Olive Green'
Carter 11
Pantone 2411C
BS 381C 277
'Cypress Green'

2 'Red Oxide'
Carter 31
Pantone 181C
BS 4800 04 C 39
'Copper Beech'

Lancashire & Yorkshire Railway

The Lancashire & Yorkshire Railway was formed in 1847 by the amalgamation of several railways, of which the Manchester & Leeds Railway was the senior, being incorporated in 1836. This line was opened from Manchester (Oldham Road) to a junction with the North Midland Railway near Leeds between 1837 and 1841. The Manchester & Bolton Railway, the Liverpool & Bury Railway and the Wakefield, Pontefract & Goole (absorbed in 1846) extended the M&LR, forming the backbone of the future Lancashire & Yorkshire Railway. Lines connecting with Preston were opened from Bolton in 1843 and from Liverpool in 1849. The independent Preston & Wyre Railway of 1840 connected Preston with the new port of Fleetwood and the rising seaside resort of Blackpool, jointly worked with the London & North Western Railway.

The L&YR's great rival was the East Lancashire Railway. This was assembled in 1846 from three railways forming an independent line eastwards from Preston through Blackburn to Colne and Todmorden, and southwards from Accrington through Bury to Clifton Junction on the Manchester & Leeds Railway near Manchester. The ELR had running powers into Manchester, a great source of friction between the companies, until it was absorbed by the L&YR in 1859.

The L&YR expanded to Halifax and Bradford, and served the growing suburban area north of Liverpool, the location of a pioneering electrification scheme in 1904. It shortened its route by cut-off lines and by close co-operation with its neighbours formed several joint lines. The total length in 1909, excluding leased or joint lines, was 527 miles.

The company's locomotive works were originally at Miles Platting in Manchester, but in 1886 they opened a new works at Horwich, near Bolton. The carriage and wagon works were at Newton Heath, Manchester.

The Lancashire & Yorkshire Railway was amalgamated with the London & North Western Railway in 1922, thereby becoming a constituent of the London Midland & Scottish Railway in 1923, and passed into the London Midland Region of British Railways in 1948.

Until 1876 the liveries of the L&YR were rather chaotic, but when Mr William Barton Wright took office as Locomotive Superintendent he took the situation in hand. 'Passenger' locomotives were painted a middle green, probably a simple chrome or Brunswick green. Lining on tenders, tanks and cabs was black, fine-lined each side with yellow. Brass beading was applied to driving wheel splashers. So-called 'mixed traffic' engines were black with red lining, but 'freight' engines were painted unlined black.

Frames were black, and rather than the more usual vermilion, inside faces, motion and all between the frames was described as a 'dark lake' or crimson. Buffer beams were vermilion and numbers were applied in gold, apparently shaded in blue. Cab interiors were buff, edged in dark brown, with the underside of the roof painted white.

Aspinall 'K2' Class 2-4-2T No. 816, built at Horwich in 1905, illustrating the earlier lettering of tank engines.
Author's collection

250
Lancashire & Yorkshire Railway

From about 1879, tender engines carried a "L&YR" monogram in gold entwined script shaded in red, and brass numberplates were introduced. These were elliptical with a broad polished border. The seriffed engine number was in the middle, in the upper border were the company initials, and in the lower border was the date of construction. During the 1880s the inner panels were apparently painted different colours to assist identification of the engine builders, for example green for Beyer, Peacock engines.

On the appointment of Mr John A.F. Aspinall in 1886, the well-known black livery was introduced, which became the standard until 1922. The black was lined with a ¾-inch vermilion [1] band, edged on the inside with a ⅛-inch white line. After a gap of 1¼ inches there was another ⅛-inch white line. Corners were incurved with a 2⅛-inch radius. Boiler bands were edged by ⅛-inch vermilion lines, with ⅛-inch white lines inside them on the bands. All 'goods' or shunting engines were lined out with red only.

The L&YR monogram continued to be used on tender locos until about 1891 when small block letters "L & Y" appeared in gold (or perhaps golden yellow) with a smaller size ampersand. Buffer beams were edged with fine black and white lines and retained numbers at first, but these were discontinued after a few years. Buffer casings were black.

Brass numberplates were retained, but the lettering changed when building started at Horwich Works. The upper border now contained "L&YR^{Y}C^O MAKERS" and the lower "HORWICH" and the date.

The company device was now used on driving wheel splashers where there was room, or on bunkers or upper cabsides. The device consisted of the arms of Lancaster and York inside a 10-inch diameter garter carrying the company name. The garter was blue on engines and tan on carriages. When on small splashers, at first the device simply cut through the lining, but by circa 1900 the lining was carried around the device in a part circle.

Mr Aspinall was promoted to be the General Manager of the L&YR in 1899, and Mr Henry A. Hoy, formerly works manager at Horwich, was appointed Chief Mechanical Engineer. In January 1901 Mr Hoy introduced "LANCASHIRE & YORKSHIRE." to tenders and tanks, tank engines having it curved over the top of the central numberplate. The 0-4-4Ts with small side tanks had "LANCASHIRE" curved over the numberplate and "YORKSHIRE." curved beneath.

251
Lancashire & Yorkshire Railway

Mr George Hughes became Chief Mechanical Engineer in 1904 and, while the treatment of tenders remained the same, altered the lettering style of tank engines to "LANCASHIRE [plate] YORKSHIRE" in a straight line. The full stop still appeared on some engines. The 0-4-4Ts retained the upper curved lettering but the lower "YORKSHIRE" was now straight. The lettering style throughout these periods was in 5-inch gold block characters, shaded to the right and below in dark blue, light blue and white. Cab interiors were now buff above waist level, but black below.

The Carriage & Wagon Superintendent at Newton Heath from 1877 to 1895 was Mr Frederick Attock, who designed the distinctive flush-panelled arc-roofed carriages that were to become the signature of L&YR trains right into the 20th century.

The standard coach livery introduced by Mr Attock consisted of a tan colour on the upright panels and top quarter panels, with 'carmine lake' on the waist panels and bottom quarter panels. The specification for the tan [2] was orange chrome 56 lbs, lemon chrome 14 lbs, burnt umber 7 lbs. By design or coincidence, this colour is identical to the typical 'teak colour' of railway paint shops.

The carmine lake [3] was specified as a base colour of oxide 56 lbs, black 4 lbs, followed by three coats of carmine lake in varnish. This method of glazing the transparent carmine over a purple brown undercoat is very similar to that of the London & North Western Railway, and the end result is much more like the 'purple lake' of that railway than the brown colour patch given in Carter's *Britain's Railway Liveries* (see next chapter for further notes). Experiments suggest that Pantone 7631C, BS 381C 449 'Light Purple Brown' would be much more accurate, and this is supported by contemporary coloured postcards. It must be said, though, that carmine is a fugitive colour, and would fade over time to a browner aspect.

Coach ends were burnt umber [4], lined in the tan colour around the outer beading and down the centre. Solebars and running gear were black. The wood centres of wheels were varnished and droplights were stained a red shade of mahogany and varnished. The mouldings surrounding the droplights and the windows were also painted burnt umber.

Unusually, roofs were zinc white rather than the lead white favoured by most railways. Nevertheless, the roofs still darkened with age and soot.

Lining on the tan and carmine livery appears to have changed over the years. Originally it is reported to have been white. The

252
Lancashire & Yorkshire Railway

Aspinall 'L1' Class 4-4-2 No. 1421 as presented in the Railway Magazine (October 1907).
Author's collection

253
Lancashire & Yorkshire Railway

A Tuck's 'Oilette' card depicting the Liverpool to Manchester express, giving a good impression of the carriage livery. — Author's collection

Aspinall 'J4' Class 4-4-0 No. 455 and a train of typical Attock-designed L&YR carriages in a posed photograph circa 1900. The locomotive is in the standard black, with the "L&Y" in small letters, that was used circa 1891 to 1901. — Author's collection

Lancashire & Yorkshire Railway

Locomotive Magazine (September 1896) states that 'a black stripe with a fine white line runs round the windows and along the middle of the carriage'. It seems that the 'black' stripe observed around the windows was actually the burnt umber, as detailed above. However, the standard lining from circa 1900 is generally taken to have been pale orange. This was apparently an optical illusion given by a thin yellow line in conjunction with a thin vermilion one. Lining was confined to around the quarter lights (windows), one line below them and another at the step change from the waist panels to the bottom quarter panels, forming a band along the waist, on the shell moulding, and on the lower edge of the door ventilators.

Carriage lettering was in a serif Roman typeface in gold. The letters were outlined with a 1/8-inch white line having a 1/8-inch red line within, a 1/8-inch gap being left between the outline and the letter through which the carmine lake showed. Class marking was shown on doors as 1ST, 2ND (abolished 1911) or 3RD.

The usual lettering of 4- and 6-wheeled vehicles was to have "L.Y.R" with square full stops to the right and the number to the left in the waist, with a device centrally below, although there were several variations. Latterly the device appeared twice, below the initials and the number.

Bogie carriages had a symmetrical arrangement, with "L.Y.R" twice, one at each end between the first two and last two compartments, and two numbers on the next waist panels inboard of the initials. There were two devices, placed below each number.

In the early 20th century, the design of bogie stock changed. Conventional beading divided the sides into bottom quarter panels, waist panels and upright panels between the windows; doors along the sides were discontinued in favour of end vestibules, and roofs were now semi-elliptical. A more extravagant, larger lettering style was introduced for the new open corridor carriages, for example the stock built for the Liverpool–Newcastle services. Open Brake Third No. 2389 featured "L.Y.R" twice in the waist panels, with the device below each. Class marking was now "THIRD CLASS" in full centrally in the waist, with the number below, actually on the bottom quarter panels. Composite carriages had "THIRD CLASS" at one end and "FIRST CLASS" at the other, with the "L.Y.R" central, and again the number below.

Lancashire & Yorkshire Railway

Non-passenger coaching stock was painted carmine lake until the 1890s, when the two-tone scheme was adopted. Body sides were finished with four coats of varnish, and ends had two coats. Lettering seems to have been a smaller version of the carriage lettering. A photograph of Diagram 108 horsebox No. 98 from the all-carmine period is lettered "3RD" on the groom's door, and "98 L.Y.R" on the drop part of the main door, all in about 3-inch characters.

General goods stock was dark grey, including solebars and buffer casings. Below the solebar was black. Brake vans were painted black with white handrails. At first the only markings were two white symbols per side, consisting of a solid equilateral triangle within a ring. From 1903, the letters "L Y" appeared, 18 inches high on most vehicles and often widely spaced. Vans had the number painted on the upper left in seriffed numerals (in the later period this was immediately over the "L" of the initials) and on the upper portion

RIGHT: Detail of L&YR carriage lettering.

256
Lancashire & Yorkshire Railway

of each end. The number plate and tare, the latter also painted in a seriffed style, were on the solebar. Vans which were vacuum-fitted had a white vee on the right-hand panel, often painted on the outside frame members, those through-piped only had a white circle. From about 1920 body numbers where they appeared were now painted in sans-serif numerals, and several open wagons started to receive them.

From about 1901 special categories of wagon were shown by colours. Refrigerated vans were white, fish vans were pale green, butter vans were pale blue, meat vans were pink and gunpowder vans were vermilion. All these had lettering and ironwork in black. This was discontinued from 1908, except for refrigerator vans.

Wagon sheets were lettered in the earlier period with the name of the company in full, but larger letters "L & Y" were adopted circa 1903. Initials with numbers placed below them in a smaller size were disposed on all four sides of the sheet. It was noted circa 1896 that 'red and white lines' also appeared. From photographs it seems that, unlike the more usual stripes diagonally across the whole sheet, a conjoined pair of stripes, one red and one white, were painted across just two opposite corners per sheet.

1 'Vermilion'
Carter 36
Pantone 485C
BS 5252 04 E 53
'Poppy Red'

2 'Tan Colour'
Carter 41
Pantone 1615C
BS 381C 439
'Leaf Brown'

3 'Carmine'
Carter 40 (approx)
Pantone 7631C
BS381C 449
'Light Purple Brown'

4 'Burnt Umber'
Carter 46
Pantone 476C
BS 4800 08 B 29
'Vandyke Brown'

The early L&YR wagon symbol.

London & North Western Railway

The L&NWR dubbed itself the 'Premier Line', with some justification as it was the largest joint-stock corporation in the world and one of its constituents was the Liverpool & Manchester Railway of 1830. The company was formed in July 1846 from an amalgamation of the Grand Junction, London & Birmingham and Manchester & Birmingham railways. There followed an expansion that created a vast empire extending from London to Carlisle and Holyhead to Cambridge, with a route mileage in 1913 of 1,802. The L&NWR was also unique in that it evolved standard liveries in the 1870s which survived unchanged for fifty years.

Because of the nature of the original companies, the L&NWR found itself with several engineering works. Responsibility for locomotive matters was divided into three regions under their own Locomotive Superintendents; the Northern Division, the Southern Division and the North Eastern Division. The old London & Birmingham Railway works at Saltley built carriages under a Carriage Superintendent. In 1857 the North Eastern Division was absorbed into the Northern Division, and from 1862 the divisions were abolished and the work of the engineering centres rationalised.

By 1865 the reorganisation was well advanced. The company's locomotive works were now solely at Crewe, which became almost as well-known as the railway itself. Established by the Grand Junction Railway, the first locomotive was built in 1843 and the site is still in railway production. Carriages were built at Wolverton, also still an active site. Wagons were built at Earlestown, near Newton-le-Willows, originally in Lancashire, now in Merseyside.

The London & North Western Railway amalgamated with the Lancashire & Yorkshire Railway in 1922, becoming a constituent of the London Midland & Scottish Railway in 1923, and passing into the London Midland Region of British Railways in 1948.

The Locomotive Superintendents include several famous names: John Ramsbottom (1842-71), James McConnell (Southern Division 1847-62), Francis Webb (1871-1903), George Whale (1903-09), C.J. Bowen Cooke (1909-20), H.P.M. Beames (1920-22) and George Hughes (1922).

Until Francis Webb took over as Locomotive Superintendent a medium green livery [1] with plain black lining was standard. However, from 1873 all engines were painted black, except two engines painted specially for the 1897 Jubilee. The famous 'blackberry' black was merely specified as drop black, the best grade of black pigment, but no different from many other railways.

A fascinating vignette of the typical L&NWR scene, with a 'Precursor' Class 4-4-0 (possibly No. 648 Archimedes) leaving Euston on the 'Scotch Express'. Author's collection

258
London & North Western Railway

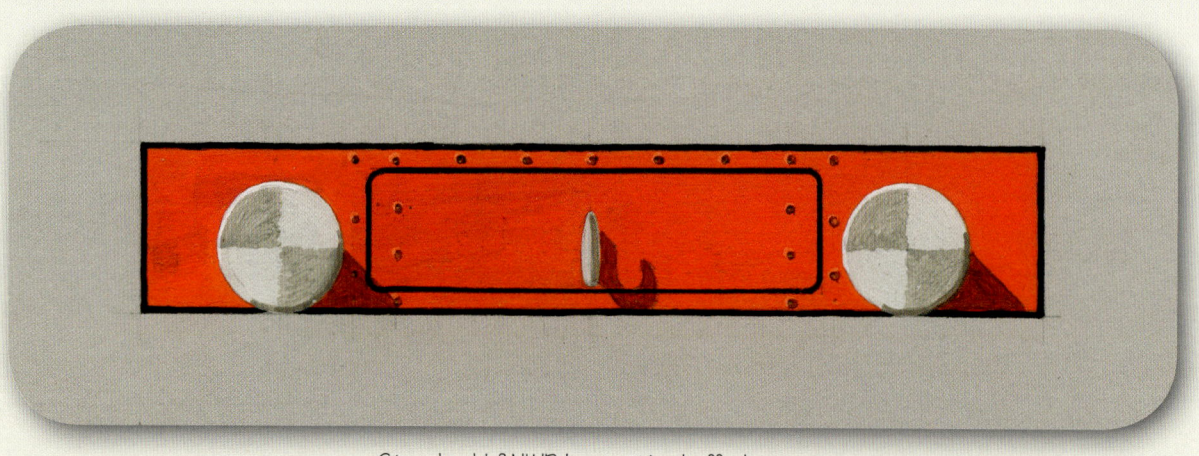

Standard L&NWR locomotive bufferbeam.

259
London & North Western Railway

Nigel J. L. Digby 1996

The high finish attained apparently lent the illusion of a distinctly lustrous blue tone to L&NWR engines.

Lining consisted of a broad ⅝-inch blue-grey line edged on the inside with a ⅛-inch white line (cream under varnish), and inside this a ¼-inch vermilion line [2]. The distance of the vermilion line from the grey was adjusted to suit conditions: 1½ inches on panels, or ½ inch on valances and around slots. On splashers the distance of the vermilion line from the edge was further in order to avoid brass nameplates, and curved round to the horizontal rather than following the shape of the splasher to a point. Boiler bands were edged with vermilion.

At first, goods engines had remained unlined, but from 1880 the 'Special DX' and '18 inch' 0-6-0s were lined and regarded as mixed traffic engines, and from 1890 all but a few engines were lined as a matter of course. All lining ceased in 1914, soon after war broke out, and was not resumed until 1921.

Bufferbeams were vermilion, except the rear bufferbeams of tenders which were always black. Vermilion bufferbeams had a black border and a line forming a rectangular panel with rounded corners between the buffers. Buffer casings were black. Cab interiors were apparently Indian red dulled with black, this mixture often being called 'purple brown'. Unusually, both inside and outside of frames were black. At one time motion was white, but from the 1890s generally all motion was left bright metal. Coupling rods

Standard L&NWR locomotive lining.

260
London & North Western Railway

'Claughton' Class 4-6-0 No. 2222 *Sir Gilbert Claughton*, built in 1913, as depicted in the *Railway Magazine*.
Author's collection

The unusual lettering on the 'Precursor Tank' Class 4-4-2Ts. *Author's collection*

London & North Western Railway

were rectangular section until the 1890s and were painted black, but thereafter fluted steel rods were introduced and these were left bright metal.

Numbers were shown originally by brass numerals on the chimney front (Mr McConnell's engines) or painted numbers on the cab sides (Mr Ramsbottom's engines). Mr Webb introduced the well-known rectangular numberplate with rounded corners. Early numberplates were cast iron, but from 1877 cast brass was used, with small "L&NWR" above the 6-inch number and "CREWE WORKS" below. Figures were polished and backgrounds were vermilion. From 1906 a new type of plate was introduced, omitting the company letters, with "CREWE WORKS" and the date below the number. From 1915 cast iron reappeared, but unlike formerly the number 6 was simply an inverted 9.

Numberplates were on the cab sides of tender engines, and the armorial device was placed in the centre of single driving wheel splashers of passenger engines, or centrally on the straight-topped splashers in use from 1905. Alone among the goods engines, the '18 inch' goods/mixed traffic 0-6-0s of 1880 also had the device, earning them the nickname 'Crested Goods' or, more irreverently, 'Cauliflowers'. The armorial device itself consisted of a red roundel containing Britannia and a lion surrounded by a great deal of gold filigree work, at a distance indeed resembling the fabled vegetable.

Tank engines had their numberplates placed in the centre of the tanks and no device, but three later classes departed from this rule. Unusually for the L&NWR, they were lettered with company initials: the 4-4-2T 'Precursor Tanks' of 1906 had "L&NWR" in 6¼-inch gold letters and featured the armorial device above the lettering; the 4-6-2T 'Prince of Wales Tanks' of 1910 had "L&NWR" in 12-inch yellow ochre letters, with the device on the upper cabside; the 0-8-2T '1185' Class shunting tanks of 1911 had "L&NWR" in 9½-inch yellow ochre letters, but no device. All this lettering was shaded red below and to the right. Numberplates were placed on the bunkers.

As well as being numbered, the passenger tender locomotives were named. The names were not very prominent, appearing in sunken black sans-serif lettering on a narrow polished brass plate. Positioned at the top of the driving wheel splasher, the nameplates followed the curve and were narrow enough to fit between the vermilion fine-lining. The circumference of the nameplate depended upon how long the name was, but on each side were standard portions bearing in very small characters on the left "L&NWRCº" and below it the month of construction, and on the right "CREWE WORKS" and the year of construction.

The nameplates on the high- and low-pressure compound engines, introduced by Mr Webb in 1884, differed slightly. The small lettering on either side of the name remained unaltered, but below was an extra radius of plate which featured the wording "F.W.WEBB'S SYSTEM". The 'Greater Britain' and 'John Hick' Class 2-2-2-2 Webb compounds were given two-word names, a word on a nameplate on both splashers, with a device below. The two plates both had the extra lower extensions but the wordings were slightly different. Both plates featured "L&NWRCº" on the left of the main word and the date of construction on the right, but the first plate had "CREWE WORKS" on the extension below, and the second "F.W.WEBB'S SYSTEM". The vermilion fine-lining was diverted around the perimeter of all these plates.

From the introduction of Mr Whale's 4-6-0 'Experiment' Class in 1905, all new passenger engines (excluding rebuilds) were built with straight combined splashers. The nameplates on these engines were also straight, but incorporated the extra portion below the name first seen on the Webb compounds, bearing the date of construction. The lettering to each side was reduced to "L&NWRCº" and "CREWE WORKS" accordingly.

Because the L&NWR was such a vast organisation, the combination of locomotives, carriages and wagons all under the same officer (as was the norm on many other railways) was not practicable, and so Wolverton Works had its own Carriage Superintendent. Mr R. Bore (1860-86) oversaw the move from Saltley to Wolverton; he was succeeded by C.A. Park (1886-1910), H.D. Earl (1910-16) and A.R. Trevithick (1916-23).

The exact date of introduction of the well-known carriage livery is a matter of conjecture, but it was standard by 1872 at the latest. Top quarter panels, upright panels and waist panels were painted a mixture called 'flake white' [3], white lead tinted with a small amount of ultramarine, which looked greenish under varnish. Bottom quarter panels, the fascia (beading) on the upper panels, and carriage ends were a dark purple brown [4], called variously 'dark claret', 'chocolate' and 'lake'. This was built up from layers, the undercoat being 'body brown', a mix of 10lb drop black and 9½lb of Indian red. The topcoat was one coat carmine lake followed by an enamel of carmine mixed with varnish. The finish was four coats

All the standard L&NWR carriage livery features are present on 50-foot Composite No. 935. *Author's collection*

London & North Western Railway

of varnish. Carmine is a true lake, made from cochineal dye on an alumina base. Being transparent, it acted like a glazing coat on the brown beneath, adding depth and lustre. Being fugitive and not light-fast, the carmine lost its violet-red tint over time.

Carriage lining was a ½-inch chrome yellow line applied to the edges of all mouldings. Between the yellow and the lake was a ⅛-inch white line. Two white lines were applied along the bottom of the body, one at each extreme end of the sides, and one outlining the top and sides of the doors above waist level. Ventilator bonnets were lake, with each louvre lined. Coach ends were unlined, with black steps and 'terracotta' colour handrails, probably Venetian red. Droplights were varnished wood and until circa 1911 fixed window mouldings were painted Venetian red to match. Thereafter the policy was to paint these the body colour. Clerestory sides, roofs and roof fittings were usually white when first painted. Underframes were painted body colour and lined until about 1890, henceforth they were plain black. Sidelamps mounted on brake van duckets were red.

From the 1870s lettering was sans-serif in gold, outlined with black, although from about 1910 gold was superseded by yellow on all but special carriages. Generally lettering was confined to carriage numbering and class marking. Smoking compartments were designated until 1903 by having "SMOKING" under the class wording, both being in small seriffed characters. After 1903 blue and white labels were applied to the right-hand compartment window. Only guard's vans with central duckets were lettered "L&NWR" on the waist moulding of the ducket. The only shaded lettering was on royal and other special saloons in red, or on West Coast Joint Stock in green.

Normally, all carriages displayed the device twice on each side and until 1910 they also carried a gold monogram of L&NWR (or WCJS), twice until 1899 but once centrally thereafter.

Non-passenger carriage stock was painted the body brown all over, and lined with the yellow and white as for the passenger vehicles. The company initials "L&NWR" and also the function of the vehicle, for example "CATTLE BOX" for prize cattle vans, were applied in the small size transfers used on other carriages.

At Earlestown, during the period under consideration, the Wagon Superintendents were J.W. Emmett (1867-1903), H.D. Earl (1903-10), A.R. Trevithick (1910-16) and W.W.H. Warneford (1916-24). Messrs Earl and Trevithick went on to become Carriage Superintendents at Wolverton (see above).

263
London & North Western Railway

Late period L&NWR wagon lettering.

London & North Western Railway

The standard colour for wagons was a medium grey [5], being an equal mix of black and white. Apparently until about 1899 it was usual to paint the outside framing of covered vans black. Refrigerator vans were white, at first with black framing but after circa 1899 all white with grey curb rail and solebar. Grey vans fitted with the automatic vacuum brake were marked with two 6-inch white diagonal stripes rising from the outer bottom corners. Vans through-piped rather than fully-fitted had only the left-hand stripe.

For many years prior to 1908, the only markings on most L&NWR goods wagons were two white diamonds 11 x 5 inches, and the solebar numberplate, although from 1882 numbers were painted on the top plank of the wagon ends. The numberplates were 13 x 6½ inches and lettered "L.N.W." at the top with the number below in 2-inch characters. Brake vans had a small B suffix after the number. Wagons for special uses had extra lettering and from 1896 it was usual to paint the maximum load of high-sided open wagons on the top plank, with the figure on the left-hand side and "TONS" on the right. Also from 1896 the numbers of cattle wagons were painted on the body side above the right-hand diamond.

From 1908 the letters "L&NWR" in 16-inch characters were used on the sides of wagons, the size reduced where space was restricted. Until 1911 the diamonds remained as well, but were largely abandoned thereafter. Load marking became usual on most stock, generally on the upper left.

Wagon sheets were lettered "L&NWR" or "LN [diamond] WR" and were marked by a diagonal cross in red.

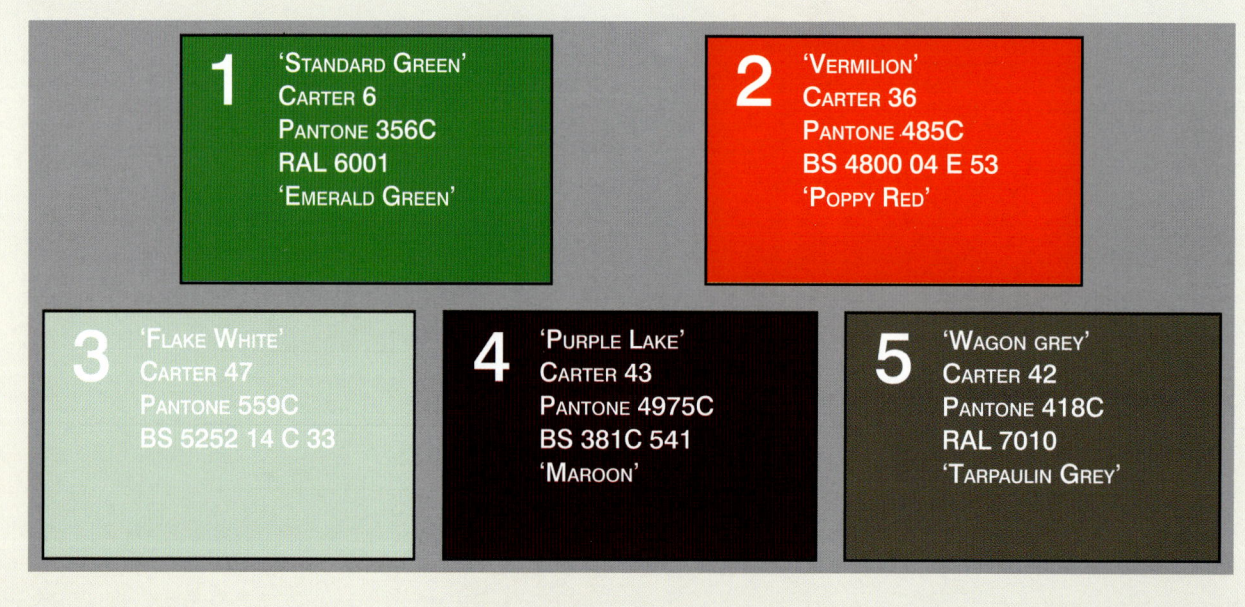

#	Name	Carter	Pantone	BS/RAL	Alt name
1	'Standard Green'	Carter 6	Pantone 356C	RAL 6001	'Emerald Green'
2	'Vermilion'	Carter 36	Pantone 485C	BS 4800 04 E 53	'Poppy Red'
3	'Flake White'	Carter 47	Pantone 559C	BS 5252 14 C 33	
4	'Purple Lake'	Carter 43	Pantone 4975C	BS 381C 541	'Maroon'
5	'Wagon grey'	Carter 42	Pantone 418C	RAL 7010	'Tarpaulin Grey'

Maryport & Carlisle Railway

This was among the oldest lines in the kingdom, being incorporated in 1837, with no less a personage than George Stephenson as its engineer. The 28 miles of the main line were without major viaducts or tunnels and so could be built relatively cheaply. The final part of the line was opened in February 1845. Although the ambitious annual dividend predicted by the directors was never achieved, a peak of 13% was reached in 1873, and in 1908 the dividend was 6%, second only to the Barry Railway and ahead of the giant London & North Western. The railway was also remarkable for retaining the name under which it was incorporated until the end of its separate existence in 1923.

The length of line owned by the M&CR was expanded to 41¼ miles by a loop line between Aspatria and Wigton opened in 1866, known as the 'Bolton Loop', and the 1867 'Derwent Branch' from Bullgill southwards to join the L&NWR line between Cockermouth and Workington, enabling the M&CR to serve Cockermouth. There was also a connection with the iron ore lines of the Cleator & Workington Junction Railway. Finally, a connection was made at Brayton with the Solway Junction Railway, a branch operated by the Caledonian Railway and intended to tap the iron ore traffic.

The success of the M&CR was built upon coal and iron ore traffic rather than passengers, although services from Maryport ran into the famous Carlisle Citadel station; annual train mileage was 194,060 for passenger trains, but 261,097 for goods and minerals. Many intermediate stations were closed to passengers comparatively early, starting in 1921. Today the main line still operates, but only Maryport, Aspatria, Wigton and Dalston stations remain open.

The Maryport & Carlisle Railway became a constituent of the London Midland & Scottish Railway in 1923, and passed into the London Midland Region of British Railways in 1948.

The Works of the railway were at Maryport. Although relatively small, they still built many of the railway's locomotives and rebuilt most of them at some point. Out of a stock of thirty-three locomotives in 1922, nearly two-thirds of their number had been designed and built at Maryport. The Locomotive Superintendents of the railway during the period under consideration were Mr Robert Campbell (1873-93), Mr William Robinson (1893-98), Mr William Coulthard (1898-1904) and Mr John B. Adamson (1904-22).

As far as can be ascertained, Maryport & Carlisle Railway locomotives were always painted green [1]. This was a darkish

Maryport & Carlisle Railway 0-4-2T No. 17, built in 1865, shows the early painted numberplate. This engine was rebuilt to an 0-6-0T in 1907.
Author's collection

266
Maryport & Carlisle Railway

chrome green, not dissimilar to that used by the Great Western. Green was applied to all of the engine, except for the smokebox, platform (footplate) and cab roof, which were black. However, most engines featured Stirling-type 'wrap over' cabs, which were all-over green. Lining was in black, fine-lined in vermilion [2], as were boiler bands. Panels on the engine and tender were edged with black, a fine line of vermilion being painted between the black and the green. Wheels were green with black tyres and axle ends, both fine-lined in vermilion.

Buffer beams were vermilion, with the engine number in large gold characters shaded with black, arranged in the usual way, e.g. "Nº [hook] 4". A number of engines had 'double' bufferbeams, incorporating a lower set of buffers to deal with chaldron wagons. By 1914 most of these had been removed, although the deep buffer planks often remained.

Although the locomotive livery remained stable, variations of numberplate and lettering occurred in certain periods. The earliest photographs indicate that engines bore large painted numbers on the centre of the lower cab panels, with a small "M & C" above, and the construction date painted below. By the 1880s, the same information was enclosed within a painted 'numberplate', an elliptical area of vermilion edged with yellow or gold. The characters

267
Maryport & Carlisle Railway

used were also yellow or gold with black shading, the number now preceded by "Nº". At this time there were still no initials on locomotives, but the words "MARYPORT & CARLISLE" had begun to appear by about 1887. The size of lettering was small, less than 6 inches, and appears to have been shaded only with black. Goods engines had no lettering.

From circa 1894 locomotives carried their numbers on brass numberplates. The letters "M & C" were arranged over the number (now just a numeral), with the date in small figures below, all on a vermilion background. Tenders and tanks now carried the initials "M & C R" in 6-inch gold characters, shaded in green and white and shadowed in black. An unusual feature was the use of 'R' before numbers to denote engines on the duplicate list, even on brass plates. Goods engines still carried no initials, and some were unlined. The numberplates used from circa 1904 omitted the date below the number. Finally, by 1920 several goods engines had received the company initials.

By 1904, the M&CR armorial device was placed on the splashers of many of the tender locomotives or the bunkers or cabs of one or two tank engines. This device was a shield without lettering or garter, bearing the arms of Maryport and Carlisle quartered with the arms of two of the railway's past chairmen.

ABOVE: M&CR 0-4-2 No. 15, built at Maryport in 1892, showing the earliest form of lettering, still combined with a painted numberplate. This engine was rebuilt in 1916, and scrapped in 1928 as LM&SR No. 10012. *Author's collection*

BELOW: A typical local train of M&CR carriages at Maryport station circa 1910. The engine had a long career, being built at Maryport in 1867 as No. 19, being placed on the duplicate list as No. R1 in 1884, and not being scrapped until 1921. *Author's collection*

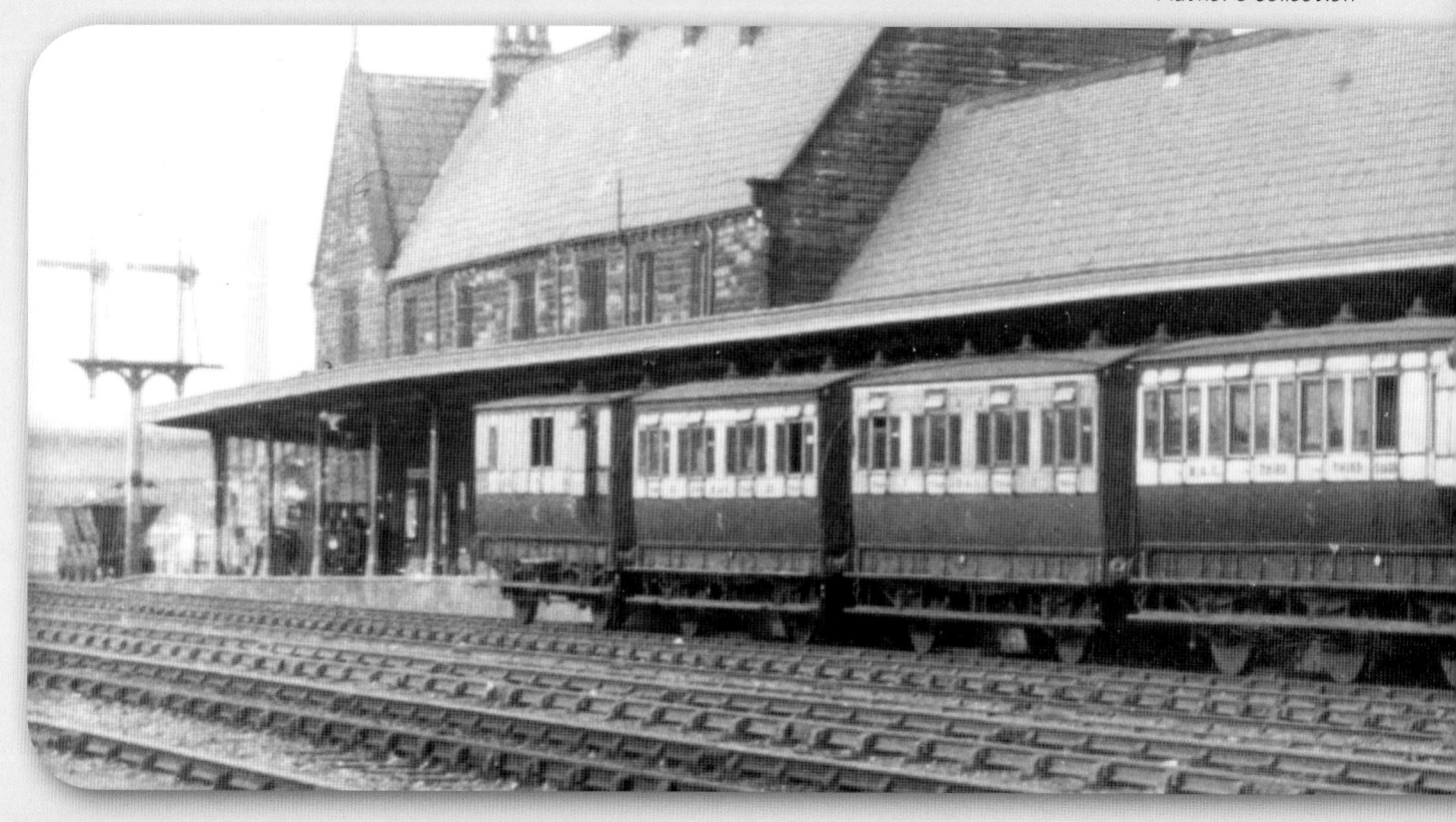

269
Maryport & Carlisle Railway

M&CR 2-4-0 No. 8, built at Maryport in 1876 and rebuilt in 1895, carries the standard Maryport & Carlisle livery, with cast brass numberplate. This engine was scrapped in 1925 as LM&SR No. 10006. Behind the engine is a rare view of a M&CR wagon, in this instance for loco coal. *Author's collection*

270 Maryport & Carlisle Railway

Originally, carriages were varnished teak, or a painted and grained equivalent. Lettering on this livery was in gold, 4 inches high, shaded in black. Class marking was in words, and the initials "M.&.C." with full stops was placed in the waist panels. There is insufficient information to indicate further markings, but below the waist it seems an early device may have featured, having a blue garter carrying the name of the company.

During 1904, as noted by the 1905 *Railway Year Book*, a new carriage livery was adopted. This was to paint the bottom quarter panels the same dark green as the engines [1]. The waist panels, upright panels and top quarter panels were white, allegedly broken slightly with green. In my opinion, this is far more likely to have been the usual paint shop practice of adding a small amount of ultramarine to the white to prevent yellowing, which looked greenish under varnish, just as on the Caledonian Railway, Furness Railway and London & North Western Railway.

The fascia or beading to the upper panels was green, as were the carriage ends and solebars. Older carriages had smaller amounts of beading than those of later designs, and so appeared to have more white on their upper parts. Lining around the mouldings was in gold ⅜-inch wide, with a fine ⅛-inch vermilion line between the gold and the green. There was also a thin vermilion line along the bottom shell moulding, just below its centre line, and some carriages had a vermilion line down each end pillar, about ½ inch in from the end. Roofs were white. Ironwork on and below the solebar was black, as were end footsteps and handrails. Droplights could be varnished wood or green.

Although green and white was the new style, older coaches in 'teak' were still to be seen. Particular mention is made of local coaches on the service to Workington remaining teak until 1912.

During the 1914-18 war, carriages going through the shops were painted green all over but still fully lined, with black ends and

Maryport & Carlisle Railway

solebars. Lining was now a yellow ochre or 'gold colour' equivalent to gold leaf. After the war the white upper panels were reinstated.

Lettering was in gold, each 3½-inch character being outlined with a thin black line. After a slight gap, through which the body colour showed, the characters were shaded with green, light green and white to right and below. The disposition of the lettering varied according to the type of carriage. Four-wheeled carriages with four compartments had "M.&.C." centrally, with device below, and two numbers placed on the panels either side of the initials. Ordinary 6-wheeled carriages tended to be lettered "M.&.C." to one side of the central door and number to the other. The device was placed on the central door. Class marking was in words on each door. However, Brake Third No. 1 and possibly others of its type were lettered differently. Here, the device was placed on the central door as usual, but the word "THIRD" was placed in the waist panels on each side. The initials were on the next panel. There being no room for the number on the waist, it was placed on the upper panels between two windows.

The 4-wheeled brake vans were lettered with the initials to the left and the number to the right of the central double doors. The device was on the leaf of the doors nearest the centre line of the body.

Bogie carriages were lettered symmetrically, with "M.&.C." centrally (always including the full stops), and two numbers, one on each side. Below each number was a device, and a script monogram of the letters "M&CR" was placed below the central initials. All class marking was in words on each door, in the same style as the other lettering.

Non-passenger stock was painted dark green all over, with ironwork in black and white roofs. A horsebox photographed circa 1900 is lettered "M.&.C." with the number below, and "LOCAL" below that. Characters were possibly yellow rather than gold, and unshaded. A horsebox photographed by its makers in 1910 carries

272
Maryport & Carlisle Railway

"M & C R" with the number below in the form "Nº 4", but there is no guarantee that this is the livery generally applied. This lettering was shaded in the same way as the passenger stock.

Goods wagons were officially classed as 'lead colour', which could be a range of greys, but in this case was a medium grey. Roofs of vans were white and ironwork below the solebar was black. Lettering was generally in about 8-inch white characters. The initials "M. &. C." were placed to the left and the number to the right of open wagons. Loco coal wagons had the word "LOCO" on the top plank of the central door. The large 10-ton open coke wagons built in 1905 were photographed by the makers with very large initials "M & C" spaced out along the side, but this may not have been the livery carried in traffic. Vans had the initials "M & C" in each panel of the door, with the number positioned centrally below.

Generally, numbers had no prefix, but a 1913 makers photo of a cattle wagon shows the usual initials on the left and the number on the right preceded by "Nº". It is not known how prevalent this was. Numbers were also painted on each end of wagons.

The standard numberplate was rectangular, with "MARYPORT &" above the central number, and "CARLISLE" below. Wagon sheets are noted as being without markings, and simply lettered "M.&.C." as usual.

| 1 | 'GREEN' CARTER 16 PANTONE 3537C BS 381C 226 'MID BRUNSWICK GREEN' | 2 | 'VERMILION' CARTER 36 PANTONE 485C BS 4800 04 E 53 'POPPY RED' |

Midland Railway (to 1906)

The Midland Railway was formed in 1844 by the amalgamation of the North Midland, Midland Counties and Birmingham & Derby railways. Centred on Derby, the original lines radiated to Leeds, Birmingham, Nottingham and Rugby via Leicester, access to London being over the London & North Western Railway. By construction of new lines and absorption of others, the Midland rapidly expanded its influence to Gloucester and Bristol, Peterborough, Lincoln, Bradford and Lancaster. Difficulties with the L&NWR prompted the Midland to build from Leicester to Hitchin, on the new Great Northern Railway, via Bedford. The first Midland trains ran into King's Cross in 1858. Congestion (and an accident) on the GNR led to the building of the Midland's own London line from Bedford to the world famous St. Pancras station, opened in 1868. At the same time the MR was driving for Manchester by extending the old branch from Ambergate to Rowsley right through the Derbyshire Peaks to Buxton and Manchester, opening in 1867. South Wales was reached by the acquisition of the Hereford, Hay & Brecon in 1869. The Midland's crowning glory was the Settle and Carlisle line across the Pennines, opened for passengers in 1876, allowing Scottish services to be run in concert with the North British and the Glasgow & South Western railways.

The Midland was a keen participant in joint lines, including the three largest: the Cheshire Lines, Midland & Great Northern and Somerset & Dorset. Over the Tottenham & Forest Gate and Tottenham & Hampstead Junction lines the MR ran to the London Tilbury & Southend Railway, which it absorbed in 1912. Total lines owned, partly owned or leased stood at 1,726 miles in 1909.

The Midland Railway became a constituent of the London Midland & Scottish Railway in 1923, and passed into the London Midland Region of British Railways in 1948.

The locomotive department, based at Derby Works, featured some of the most famous names in railway history: Matthew Kirtley (1844-73), Samuel Waite Johnson (1873-1903), Richard Mountford Deeley (1904-09) and Henry Fowler (1909-23), each having an effect on the livery styles.

During the Kirtley era, locomotives were dark Brunswick green [1], including frames. Smokeboxes, footplates, guard irons and steps were black, buffer beams and inside faces of frames were vermilion, and interiors of cabs were brown. It appears that the earliest lining was a black band only, and panels of lining had incurved corners. Tenders and the majority of tanksides were given three panels. White fine-lining appeared in the late 1860s. Generally, engine numbers were in brass cut-out numerals on the centre line of boilers below the domes.

There were at first few changes after S.W. Johnson took over as Locomotive Superintendent, but brass numerals were removed from boilers to cab sidesheets or rear driving wheel splashers, except

Smith-Johnson Compound 4-4-0 No. 2632, the second of a class of five introduced in 1901, as presented in the Railway Magazine (November 1903). This locomotive was renumbered No. 1001 in 1907. *Author's collection*

274
Midland Railway (to 1906)

on many of the Kirtley 2-4-0s where the large outside springs made this position impossible. Lining was in black, fine-lined in white, tenders having two panels of lining with ordinary rounded corners. Generally side tanks and cab side sheets were only edged with black and white, but panels of lining were sometimes applied. The most significant change came in 1876 when a lighter green [2] was adopted for locomotives. A specification of 1880 shows that frames, sandboxes and guard irons were painted brown, lined in white. Front and rear buffer beams were lettered "M [hook] R" in 6-inch gold sans-serif characters shaded in blue and black.

The Midland dark red [3], often inexactly termed 'crimson lake', was not officially adopted for locomotives until November 1883, although the last new engine appeared in green in July. The actual pigment used for the red livery was alizarin crimson, made from the coal-tar derivative anthracene, discovered in 1868. Because of its transparent nature, the alizarin had to be combined with a coloured undercoat. In 1894, after the iron oxide surface preparation, two coats of iron oxide and crimson lake were followed by three coats of varnish. Another formula of 1895 was four coats of purple brown followed by one coat of purple brown and crimson, and five coats of varnish. 'Iron oxide' and 'purple brown' were probably equivalent terms.

Lining was black and lemon chrome yellow [4], panelled on tenders but as edging on other sheets and tanks, and around the base of the dome, a practice dating from the earlier period. The MR initials were in use on tenders and tanks by 1892, seriffed in gold, shaded in blue, white and black. On tanksides, the lettering flanked the central brass numbers. Mr Johnson standardised the brass numerals as 6½ inches high, the 3 having a flat top until 1897.

Other details, such as the areas painted black, remained the same as previously in the green period. Buffer beams were vermilion [5] edged in black and yellow, and still featured "M [hook] R" in gold letters shaded in blue and black. During 1898, rear buffer beam lettering was moved up onto the body; it also became usual to paint the tops of splashers black.

From the early 1880s the armorial device appeared on the driving wheel splashers where there was room. It consisted of the Arms of Birmingham, Derby, Bristol, Leicester, Lincoln and Leeds on a shield, surrounded by a scroll bearing the company name, all within a 14 x 13½-inch diamond shape of decoration.

When Richard Deeley succeeded Mr Johnson in 1904, the panels of lining on tenders were abandoned and eventually engines were finished in a simplified form of the earlier livery, dealt with in the next chapter.

275
Midland Railway (to 1906)

Standard Midland Railway bufferbeam lettering.

Midland Railway (to 1906)

From 1844 carriages were painted 'claret', very possibly the same colour as the later crimson, but it is believed that Third class vehicles were dark green. By the 1870s, when Thomas Clayton became Carriage Superintendent, the livery that was to survive until the end of the company was in place.

Carriage sides and ends were painted crimson; after surface preparation, there was a coat of 'lake ground' (probably the same iron oxide or purple brown used for the engines), followed by crimson lake, then crimson in varnish (an enamel). The fascia (beading) was painted black, then there was a coat of varnish, followed by lettering and lining. Lining was in gold ¼-inch wide, bordered by a ⅛-inch vermilion line between the gold and the black, but the black mouldings on coach ends were not lined. The final treatment was three coats of varnish.

The many layers of treatment repeated on several occasions over a carriage's life could lead to a considerable depth of paint on the mahogany panels beneath. When researching old carriage bodies grounded in Norfolk, I came across ex-Midland Railway 6-wheeled Brake Third No. 64 (later M&GN No. 178). The owning family's young son had kicked his football hard against the carriage and at the point of impact the paint layers had shattered like glass. The shards of paint were at least ⅛ inch thick and the crimson lake layers were still glossy. On other grounded bodies I have observed the gold lining, when revealed in a similar way, to still be bright. Truly the Midland ensured that their carriage livery endured.

Roofs and roof fittings were lead grey, but the outside faces of rainstrips are thought to have been crimson. Solebars were crimson, and until 1902 were bordered in black, lined yellow and vermilion, but after which time they were painted a plain red-brown.

Lettering was in gold sans-serif characters, shaded in red and white and shadowed in black. From the 1880s, a standard style was adopted for both 6-wheeled and bogie vehicles, with 2½-inch

Midland Railway (to 1906)

lettering in the waist only. Class marking was in words on the doors as "FIRST" or "THIRD", Second class having been abolished by the Midland in 1875.

The position of company initials depended on the design of the carriage. Where a vacant waist panel was central, it was usual to have "M.R" (with full stop) in the centre, flanked by two numbers as symmetrically as possible, for example "[THIRD] 874 [THIRD] M.R [THIRD] 874 [THIRD]". Where there was a door at or near the centre, the two letters were separated on each side of the door, for example "[THIRD] 1217 [THIRD] M [THIRD] R [THIRD] 1217 [THIRD]". Bogie vehicles were treated in exactly the same way, albeit with more doors appended to each end, and with greater spacing of the components.

Note that where there was a guard's or luggage compartment at one end of the vehicle, it was not included in the calculations for where the 'centre' of the carriage lay. Aside from the lettering "LUGGAGE", this part of the vehicle was ignored. Thus, as can be seen in the accompanying painting, even though 6-wheeled Brake Third No. 865 literally had a central door, the lettering was prepared as if there were a blank central panel.

The 4-wheeled passenger brake vans were lettered on the ducket. The two upright panels had an initial apiece, for example "M [beading] R", with the number in the waist panel below. On these vehicles, "LUGGAGE" was used on one of each pair of luggage compartment doors. Interestingly, the Midland did not ever mark the guard's door on any of its carriages.

The device was featured only on Firsts and Composites. All of these vehicles had two devices; 6-wheeled Composites featured them on the First class doors, and 6-wheeled Firsts and bogie Composites had them below the two numbers.

There were a number of special carriages such as sleeping carriages, officer's inspection carriages, family saloons or invalid carriages, and

278
Midland Railway (to 1906)

The quintessential Midland Railway scene, at Gloucester. The card was posted in 1911.   Author's collection

Johnson '6' Class 0-4-4T No. 1636, illustrating the standard tank engine livery. This engine was built in 1883, became No. 1290 in 1907, and was withdrawn as BR No. 58044 in 1948.   Author's collection

Midland Railway (to 1906)

these tended either to have the initials and number close together in the centre of the vehicle, for example "M.R.470", with two devices situated symmetrically on the bottom quarter panels on each side, or alternatively to have one set of initials and one number spaced out on the side, for example "M.R   439", with a device below each.

In 1897 the famous clerestory carriages with right-angled corners to the fascias were introduced. For the first time mouldings were provided to the doors below the waist, and these were painted black and lined in the usual way. Clerestory sides were crimson, apparently fully lined out. Generally, the area between rainstrip and cornice was painted black and varnished.

Clerestory stock lettering differed considerably from the arc-roofed stock. All waist lettering was now in 3-inch sans-serif characters. Class marking was still in words on the waist panels of the doors, but the word "MIDLAND" was used instead of the initials. This occurred once centrally on 6-wheeled carriages and twice on bogie coaches. The device appeared below each occurrence of the name, even on Thirds, until this was stopped after 1898. All numbers were in the upper panels in a smaller 2-inch size, two numbers being arranged symmetrically, on bogie vehicles as near as possible above the "MIDLAND" wording.

There were a number of special carriages which had additional lettering such as "DINING CARRIAGE", usually between the two "MIDLAND" positions.

Non-passenger carriage stock was painted as for passenger vehicles, although lining was in yellow. Lettering was also in the same style with "M.R" and the number usually in the waist. Special vehicles often had their use denoted, for example "MILK VAN", "MEAT VAN", "STORES VAN" or "FISH TRUCK". Horseboxes had "M.R" and the number below placed centrally on the drop part of the door.

Wagons were always light lead grey, with everything black below the solebar. The paint consisted of 112 lb white lead, 4 lb black, plus the liquid medium. The white lead was sensitive to sulphur in the atmosphere and so the grey darkened over time.

Originally the only mark of ownership was the solebar numberplate, which was a rectangle 13¾in x 7⅜in with incurved corners, simply lettered "MIDLAND" with the number below. From the early 1880s the large letters "MR" were introduced using a special "self-cleaning" white oxalic paint. At first, 21-inch letters were applied only to open wagons, tariff vans and brake vans. The latter two had additional numbers prefixed "M." on the body side,

Standard brake van lettering.

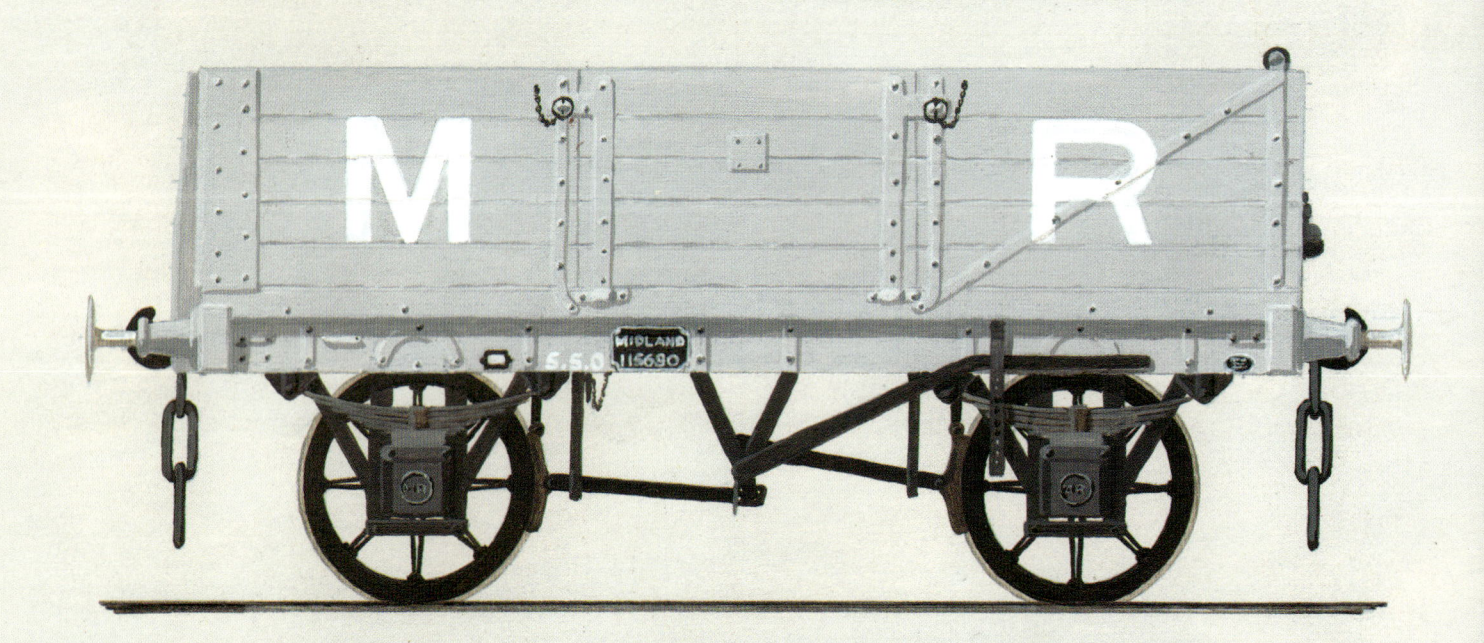

280
Midland Railway (to 1906)

white on a black background surrounded by a white border; tariff vans had a plain rectangle, brake vans had a rectangle with incurved corners.

During the early 1890s it became the custom to paint the initials on cattle wagons. They were commonly lettered with the initials and size on either side of the central doors "MR [door] LARGE", but the final style placed the initials on either side, for example "LARGE M [door] R 17890".

Other vans received initials a few years later. Most vans were outside-framed with sliding doors; these were lettered in 12½-inch initials on the doors, with the number above. There were many types of special vans, those with outside frames often had the 12½-inch initials on the left of the central doors, but those with plain sides used the large initials.

Wagon sheets were lettered "M.R.Co" until about 1900, from when "M.R" was used. Lettering was seriffed and 18 inches high, with 12-inch numbers below. In the 1890s sheets reportedly had yellow borders.

1 'Dark Brunswick Green'
Carter 19
Pantone 3435C
BS 381C 227
'Deep Brunswick Green'

2 'Light Green'
Carter 14
Pantone 349C
RAL 6001
'Emerald Green'

3 'Alizarin Crimson'
Carter 28
Pantone 188C
BS 381C 540
'Crimson'

4 'Lemon Chrome'
Carter (none)
Pantone 116C
BS 5252 10 E 55
'Canary Yellow'

5 'Vermilion'
Carter 36
Pantone 485C
BS 5252 04 E 53
'Poppy Red'

Midland Railway (1906-22)

The Midland Railway was formed in 1844 by the amalgamation of the North Midland, Midland Counties, and Birmingham & Derby Railways. The company's history is covered in the previous chapter.

Crimson had been introduced on Midland locomotives in 1883. The pigment used was alizarin crimson, which due to its transparency had to be combined with a coloured undercoat. The method of application in the years under discussion in this chapter was a lead grey base, followed by an undercoat of 75% iron oxide 25% alizarin, and a topcoat of 75% alizarin 25% iron oxide. There were then four coats of varnish.

Mr Richard M. Deeley took over from Mr Johnson in 1904, and began simplifying the Johnson livery. This involved abandoning the bands of lining on tenders, but retaining the initials "M R". Finally, a new Deeley style discarding the initials in favour of large numbers was in general use from the end of 1906.

The body colour remained crimson, lined in black and fine-lined in lemon chrome, but the amount of lining was much reduced. Tanks and bunkers were still edged in black, fine-lined yellow, but the only boiler bands lined were those by the cab and smokebox, and then only on the edges adjacent to the boiler.

Cab sides and cab fronts had formerly been lined on the front corners, but now this was omitted, the edging at top and bottom being carried round onto the cab front. Engines with rounded eaves to the cab roofs had no lining on the cab front at all.

Splashers often had any brass beading painted black, and a black edge fine-lined yellow followed the perimeter. Valances were crimson, edged black and yellow on the lower edge only. The beading around the edge of Johnson-designed tenders was painted black, ignoring the central vertical strip, and lined with a single yellow line on the inside edge between the black and the crimson. The outside tender frames were crimson, the lower edges and the frame holes being lined with black and yellow.

Wheels were black, a yellow line being taken around the inner edge of the tyres. Inside frames were black, except on the inside-cylinder 4-4-0s, where the front portion of the frames above the bogies was still crimson and lined in black and yellow. Outside frames continued to be crimson, again lined in black and yellow. Outside cylinders were crimson, lined fore and aft with black and yellow, and had polished steel cylinder covers. Fluted coupling rods had the central portion painted black.

The brass numerals and company initials "M R" on tenders were abandoned, and the engine number was applied in large 18-inch gold numerals (14-inch on smaller panels) in a seriffed style, shaded in black. The smokebox door carried a rectangular black numberplate, on which the numbers appeared in polished steel.

Bufferbeams were unaltered, being vermilion edged in black and yellow, with the initials transferred onto the front beams in the form "M [hook] R". These were normally sans-serif, but seriffed versions appeared from time to time. Rear bufferbeams were not lettered, and the practice of placing the initials on the rear of tenders or bunkers was dropped.

A larger new armorial device replaced the old diamond-shaped one, and was transferred on cabsides. The new device still featured

Fowler '483' Class 4-4-0 No. 483, as shown in the *Railway Magazine* in 1913. This class of engine was nominally a superheated rebuild by Fowler of Johnson's '1740' Class of 1885-87, but in reality very little material was reused. Author's collection

Midland Railway (1906-22)

New standard cabside device and lining on passenger tender engines.

the Arms of Birmingham, Derby, Bristol, Leicester, Lincoln and Leeds on a shield, but the filigree work was now omitted. The shield was supported by two mythical sea creatures and surmounted by the wyvern, with a white and blue scroll below featuring the simple word "MIDLAND" in black.

The new Deeley livery was applied to most engines, whether they were vacuum-braked and capable of passenger working, or just steam-braked goods engines. Tank engines lagged a little behind tender engines in the application of the new livery, and differed in that they had 14-inch numerals, and did not receive the new device. The '2000' Class 0-6-4Ts were the exception to this rule, having 18-inch numerals and the device on the bunkers. No lining was applied to the valances and steps of tank engines.

The simplified livery was introduced in stages, the first evidence in 1904 being the abandonment of tender lining panels as noted above. A further complication was the renumbering of the whole locomotive stock in 1907, resulting in a large variety of hybrids, common ones being the old numbers in large numerals on the new livery, or new numbers in brass numerals on the old livery.

283
Midland Railway (1906-22)

Large numbers and Deeley lining style as applied to Johnson tenders.

Midland Railway (1906-22)

Early in Mr Deeley's time there were several experiments to reduce expenditure on unfitted goods locomotives. There were apparently engines running in unlined crimson, or alternatively 'locomotive brown' (just the iron oxide or purple brown undercoat) lined in black. These examples remained unaltered for some time. Generally, goods engines assumed the simplified crimson livery, but without lining below the footplate. There are also reported examples of plain black.

Mr Deeley resigned in 1909, to be replaced by Mr (later Sir) Henry Fowler. From this time, the policy for all goods engines, whether fitted or unfitted, was to paint them plain black. Tender engines still had the device on the cab side.

The Carriage & Wagon department had been under the control of David Bain since 1902. The basic carriage livery remained crimson, with fascias (beading) painted black. Lining was in gold around the edges of the fascia, with a thin vermilion line between the gold and the black. Solebars, which had formerly been lined crimson, were now painted plain red-brown, possibly Indian red. Below the solebar was black, except the wooden centres of Mansell wheels, which were also red-brown. From about 1912 solebars were painted black.

The major change was to the lettering style, carried out during 1906. The old style had used the initials "M.R" on arc-roofed stock with two numbers positioned symmetrically on either side, or "MIDLAND" on the square-panelled clerestory stock with numbers halfway up panels between windows, all in sans-serif gold characters shaded in red and shadowed in black. The new style abandoned this practice in favour of a large "MIDLAND" in the eaves panels, using 4-inch-high bold seriffed lettering in unshaded gold. The square-panelled clerestory carriages had to have a section of the eaves moulding made deeper to take the new transfers. Black was the desired background, and on the older arc-roofed carriages and the new Bain clerestories, a rectangle of black was provided on the otherwise crimson top quarter panel. A position as near central to the carriage as possible was used. The 6-wheeled arc-roofed stock retained its former lettering, as did most of the 6-wheeled clerestory vehicles.

Carriage numbers were in the waist panels of most stock, except the square-panelled clerestories which retained the positions on the upright panels for some time, before being placed on the waist. Class marking, formerly in words on the waist panel of each door, now became 8-inch seriffed gold numerals on the lower door

RIGHT: Deeley '999' Class 4-4-0 No. 999, built in 1907, in the simplified Deeley livery. Note the area of lined crimson on the main frames above the bogie, and the position of the lettering on the deep bufferbeam. The small brass power class number introduced in 1905 can be seen on the upper part of the cab. *Author's collection*

285
Midland Railway (1906-22)

286
Midland Railway (1906-22)

panels. All lettering and numbering other than the "MIDLAND" in the eaves was shaded in red and shadowed in black. The device was no longer used.

From about 1912, the beading on doors below the waist of square-panelled clerestory stock was painted crimson and not lined, and it is believed that during the First World War, lining became yellow rather than gold. New stock in 1921 was still lettered "MIDLAND" in the eaves, but now in a sans-serif style, shaded in the same way as the other lettering.

Wagons saw no alteration from the pre-1906 period. Light lead grey was applied to the bodies and solebars of most wagons, with black below the solebar. The initials "M R" were used on all wagons, the largest size being retained for open wagons, tariff vans and brake vans. From January 1909, brake vans running over the congested central main lines of the system carried racks into which large identifying letters were inserted for train control purposes.

From 1913 the original rectangular numberplates with incurved corners were replaced on new wagons by a different design. This featured "MIDLAND" cast along a straight top but had a semi-elliptical bottom edge, with the number curved to follow it. From 1917, numbers began to appear on the bodies of open wagons, on the left-hand side under the "M". Finally, in the last few years before grouping, the Midland purchased a quantity of war surplus grey paint which was used on repaired wagons, leaving them a darker colour.

Service vehicles were mostly light grey, but engineering department dropside wagons were painted red oxide and lettered "ED". Ballast brakes and snow ploughs were also red oxide.

Lettering of an Engineering Department ballast wagon.

North Staffordshire Railway

The North Staffordshire Railway, or the 'Knotty' as it was generally known, was first promoted as the Potteries Railway, proposed in 1835 to link Stoke-on-Trent with the Grand Junction Railway, but shelved in 1837. The Manchester & Birmingham Railway would also have had a route passing right through the Potteries, but opposition from the GJR curtailed the original line at Macclesfield. During the Railway Mania of 1845 there were many schemes for Staffordshire, but disagreement between the larger railways prevented most of them being promoted. This cleared the ground for a revival of the Potteries Railway as the Staffordshire Potteries Railway. Competition for the district was reduced by amalgamations with the Churnet Valley and the Derby & Crewe schemes, and the North Staffordshire Railway was incorporated in 1845. The NSR came to an agreement with the Trent & Mersey Navigation (opened 1777), whereby the railway managed the canal and guaranteed an annual income. Construction of the railway began in 1847 and the first section opened in 1848.

The Knotty expanded and consolidated into a densely-packed system of lines centred on Stoke, extending to Macclesfield in the north, Crewe in the west, near Stafford in the south and to the Midland Railway near Derby in the east. Through services included trains from Manchester to Stafford, and from Nottingham and Derby to North Wales. The length of lines owned or partly owned in 1908 was 225½ miles, including 10 miles joint with the Great Central and the 8 miles of the 2ft 6ins gauge Leek & Manifold Valley Light Railway.

The engineering works of the railway were established in 1864 at Stoke. The first locomotives were constructed in 1868, and by the beginning of the 20th century most of the locomotives and rolling stock of the railway were being built there. Locomotive Superintendents in the period under review were Mr Charles Clare (1875-82), Mr Luke Longbottom (1882-1903), Mr John Adams (1903-15) and Mr John Hookham (1915-23).

The North Staffordshire Railway became a constituent of the London Midland & Scottish Railway in 1923, and passed into the London Midland Region of British Railways in 1948.

Under Mr Clare, locomotives were painted Brunswick green, lined out with black and white in edgings and panels in a very similar manner to the contemporary livery of the Midland Railway. On tenders and driving wheel splashers or tanksides was the 'Staffordshire Knot' in gold, with limited shading in blue. Numberplates were small and elliptical in brass with "NORTH

North Staffordshire Railway '38' Class 2-4-0 No. 39, built at Stoke in 1874 and shown here in the March 1901 *Railway Magazine* as rebuilt by Mr Longbottom with a larger boiler. The engine is painted in the standard Longbottom livery.
Author's collection

North Staffordshire Railway

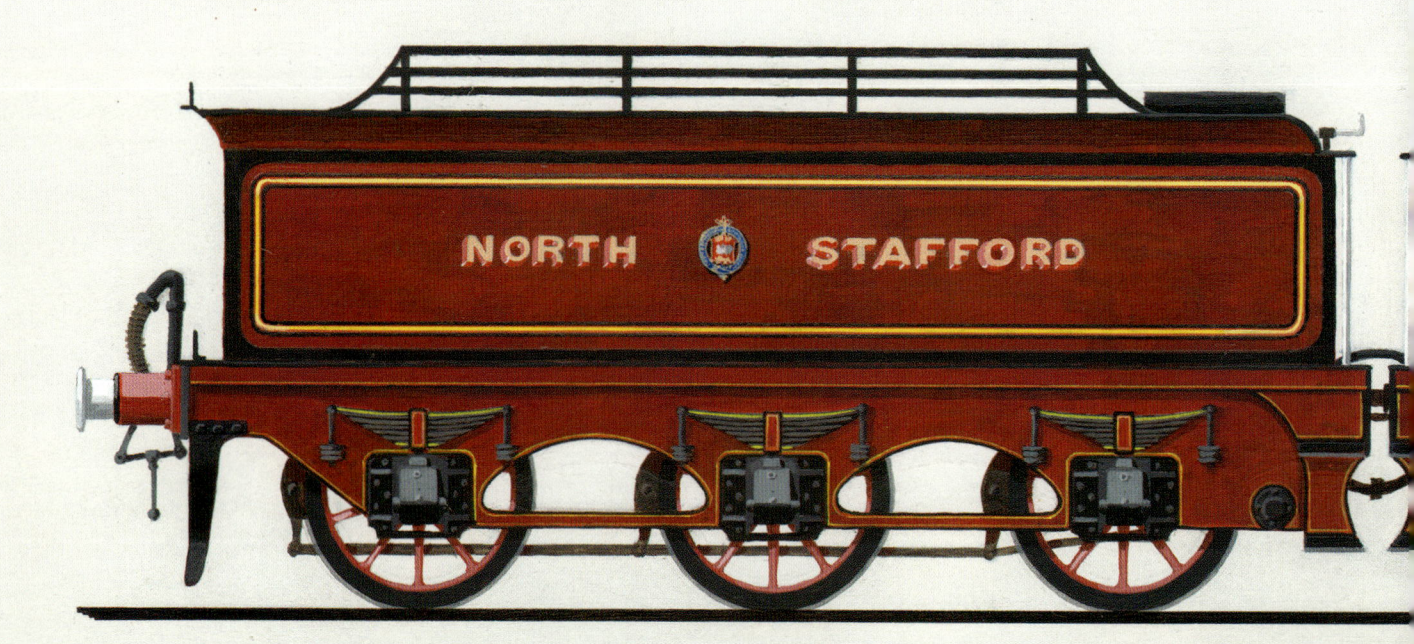

STAFFORDSHIRE" above the seriffed central number and "RAILWAY" below on a vermilion background, placed on cabsides or bunkers, and lined around. By 1880, use of this plate on new construction had been dropped, and a very small elliptical plate carrying the maker's name and the building date was placed in the same position. Buffer beams were vermilion [1] edged in black and white. The engine number appeared on the buffer beams, for example "Nº [hook] 19" in large seriffed gold characters, shadowed to right and below in brown.

Mr Luke Longbottom became locomotive superintendent at the end of 1882, and in 1883 extended to locomotive use the dark reddish brown, recorded as 'Victoria' brown, already being applied to the carriage stock, bringing a pleasing uniformity to the trains. This was probably an iron oxide or purple brown. From a contemporary illustration in the *Railway Magazine* (March 1901), this colour would appear to correspond with colour patch No. 38 in E.F. Carter's *Britain's Railway Liveries*, or BS 381C 412 'Dark Brown', Pantone 4625C.

Lining was now in black and yellow in the same style as before, but where there were panels of lining, a thin vermilion line was applied a short distance (about 2 inches) within the panel. Boiler bands were black, edged yellow, with a vermilion line at the same

North Staffordshire Railway

distance to each side on the boiler clothing. The armorial device was now placed on driving wheel splashers and in the middle of tanks, leaving only tenders to be adorned by the 'knot'.

The company device incorporated the arms of Stoke, surrounded by a green (later blue) gilt-edged garter on which the words "NORTH STAFFORDSHIRE RAILWAY COMPANY" in Gothic script appeared. The arms were 'tied' to the garter at the top by a traditional Staffordshire knot.

In 1902 Mr John H. Adams, son of the famous William Adams of the L&SWR, was appointed Locomotive Superintendent. In the following year he introduced possibly one of the strangest liveries of all the pre-grouping railways. The new style was first noted in the *Locomotive Magazine* of 24th October 1903. The base colour was changed to a shade known as 'madder lake' [2], a crimson similar to the Midland colour, but apparently browner. Unfortunately no specification has survived. It seems that this colour may have already been applied to the carriage stock of the railway for some years (see below).

The pigment 'crimson madder' had been made for centuries from the root of the common madder plant *Rubia tinctorum*, which contained the anthraquinone compounds alizarin and purpurin. When alizarin was successfully synthesised in 1868, paint makers

North Staffordshire Railway

North Staffordshire Railway 'E' Class 0-6-0 No. 74 of 1874, the fourth engine to be built at Stoke, pictured as rebuilt in 1895 with a larger boiler. The vermilion inner line of the Longbottom livery shows up well on the original print. Note the bufferbeam lettering.
Author's collection

on the whole switched to it in favour of the natural product, and the growing of the madder plant (mostly in Holland) largely died out.

The original madders could be produced in a wide range of reds, but crimson madder was a rich crimson, and so it is puzzling why the 'madder lake' of the NSR should apparently be of a browner hue than the crimson of the Midland. Certainly, the few contemporary reports of North Staffordshire Railway locomotives all use the expression 'crimson lake'. That being said, there was a commercially-available pigment (*Paint and Colour Mixing* by A.S. Jennings promotes Lewis Berger's 'permanent crimson madder'), which does indeed have a slightly browner aspect than alizarin crimson. Being a transparent pigment, the preparation coats applied underneath the top colour would also have had their effect. The coloured illustrations in the *Railway Magazine* (March 1904 and December 1907) and the only known contemporary colour postcard tend to confirm the slight brownish nature of the crimson madder.

I cannot say I am particularly happy with the colour references given in the literature, and I believe that when, eventually, a specification is discovered, the result will be more like Carter No. 28 (Pantone 188C, BS 381C 540 'Crimson') than is generally supposed.

Most of the engine was painted madder lake, including tender frames. Smokeboxes, platforms (footplates), tank tops, tops of sandboxes and cab roofs were black. Locomotive frames were black, but above the footplate were madder lake. Wheels were madder lake, with black tyres and axle ends. Buffer beams were vermilion lined with black and yellow, but buffer shanks were madder lake. The former seriffed bufferbeam lettering was maintained, but the dot below the "o" was replaced by a dash.

Perhaps the oddest feature of the Adams livery was the lining. It may have been a conscious decision to differentiate the engines of the NSR from those of the Midland, their colours being so similar. The main colour was pale yellow (lemon chrome), and this was bordered by black in a complete reversal of any conventional style. Between the black and the yellow was a thin line of vermilion. A further peculiar feature, and not one generally realised because it rarely shows up well on orthochromatic photographs, was that on the larger body panels there was a broad border of black, about 3 inches wide, which followed the corners and curves of the main lining, which was itself 3 inches away from this border. All the smaller panels also had a black border, but narrower in proportion.

291
North Staffordshire Railway

The Adams livery on 'M' Class 0-4-4T No. 9, built December 1907 and presented in the *Railway Magazine* of that month. The bunker is shown with straight sides, but after a short while in traffic a flared top was added to increase capacity.

Author's collection

RIGHT: Standard locomotive lining 1903-22.

Tender sides and rear, bunker sides and rear, tanksides and full-height cabsides had the wide border of black. At the front end of tanks, the border was taken around the curve, so that the front faces of the tanks seem to have been entirely black, or perhaps have a central portion of unlined madder lake. On the main panels, after a gap of the body colour, were the broad bands of lining. The dimensions of the main lining seem to have been 1½ inches of yellow, edged on each side with ⅛ inch vermilion, then 1⅜ inches black, making a band 4½ inches wide. Boiler bands were madder lake, lined on the outer edge with yellow, having a further band of black (approximately one inch wide) painted on the boiler clothing. Between the yellow and the black was the fine-line of vermilion. The bases of the dome and safety valve cover were lined in black, with the vermilion and yellow on the upper edge only.

Other areas such as cab fronts, upper parts of cabs (such as on tank engines), splashers and sandboxes were lined in a compressed version of the main lining. Here, the yellow lining was applied directly to the wide black edging, again with a vermilion line between. Splasher beading was painted black with the vermilion and yellow lines adjacent, the remaining edges of the splasher

292
North Staffordshire Railway

outside the yellow being black. Below the footplate, valances and steps were also edged with black, vermilion and yellow.

Tenders and tanksides carried the company name in the form "NORTH [device] STAFFORD" in 5-inch gold sans-serif letters, shaded in vermilion and white to left and below, and shadowed in black. Because of the unequal length of the words, the device was not central. The knot was no longer used, except on one of the 4-4-0s of 1910, No. 87, which had it on the driving wheel splashers.

The first engine in madder lake, apparently 2-4-0 No. 14 after its rebuild in September 1903, had its number applied in seriffed brass numerals. The first batch of new engines in madder lake (the 'L' Class 0-6-2T of December 1903) had a strange cast brass 'knot' numberplate, but this was not used again. Gold seriffed transfers became the standard numerals, shaded in the same manner as the main lettering.

The earlier carriages of the North Staffordshire Railway were standardised at 20 feet in length, 4-wheeled with arc roofs and perpendicular ends, squared corners to the fascias (beading) and a deep waist panel, and altogether were rather reminiscent of early Great Northern Railway carriages. By 1880, vehicles 26 feet long were being produced, still 4-wheeled, but with a 'turn-under' at each end as well on each side, which became the standard.

293
North Staffordshire Railway

The carriages were originally 'claret', but from 1875 'Victoria' brown was applied to the bottom quarter panels, with white in the upright and top quarter panels, extended in 1882 to the waist panels as well. The fascias were brown, as were solebars and carriage ends. Lining was a gold line around the fascia, with a fine white line between the gold and the brown. Door ventilators were lined on each louvre with gold, fine-lined vermilion, giving a striped effect on photographs.

From about 1890, the design of NSR carriages changed dramatically. New vehicles were 6-wheeled and 35 feet 6 inches long, with brake vans, saloons and carriages for branch line use at 29 feet 3 inches. The panelling was altered, dispensing with waist and upper quarter panels except on the doors, and becoming virtually identical to carriages of the London & North Western Railway.

Carriage lettering was in gold sans-serif characters, described in *Moore's Monthly Magazine* (December 1896) as being 'outlined with blue', which would have given it definition against the white panels. Photographs suggest that there was actually blue shading as well. Class marking was in words on each door. Lettering varied, but in general the number appeared twice in the waist inboard of the end compartments and the device was placed centrally on the bottom quarter panels. At left of centre on the waist was "NSR" in gold script lettering, with a 'knot' in the corresponding position on the right.

From 1896 the white upper panels, which apparently weathered badly in the Potteries atmosphere, were abandoned. It had been thought that carriages were now painted all-over brown, but it is clear from an interview with Mr William Douglas Phillips, the General Manager, in the *Railway Magazine* (February 1899) that this was not so. He states: 'We have recently altered the colour of our coaches. They are now painted a bright lake colour'. I believe that this almost certainly indicates the adoption of a crimson livery, probably the 'madder lake', anticipating the locomotives by several years. Nevertheless, this point requires further clarification.

Certainly by 1903 the madder lake was being used. The edges of the fascia were lined in gold, possibly fine-lined in vermilion. Solebars at this date may well have been madder lake, and roofs and wheel tyres were white.

The lettering style on main-line carriages remained the same as in the earlier period, with class marking in words on the waist panel of each door, the number appearing at each end and the device central on the lower panels. The transfers supplied were gold characters, apparently now shaded in red. At left of centre in the waist panels was "NSR" in gold script lettering, with a 'knot' in the corresponding position on the right. Because of the L&NWR-type panelling, the lettering could not sit centrally between the doors, and so, to the left of centre, the number and the script "NSR" were placed on the panels immediately to the right of a door, and to the right of centre, the knot and the number were placed immediately to the left of a door.

The 6-wheeled full brakes, which featured many upright panels and a central ducket in the L&NWR manner, nevertheless followed the rules and were numbered in the central panel of each end section, with the script "NSR" to the right of the left-hand pair of doors, and the knot to the left of the right-hand pair of doors. The guard's door immediately to the right of the ducket carried "GUARD" in the waist panel and had the device below.

Bogie carriages 49 feet long began appearing from Stoke Works in 1906, at first with the usual arc roof, but from 1908 with a new semi-elliptical 'cove' roof. Solebars were now painted black.

An unusual aspect to NSR carriages was the retention of white (cream under varnish) on the waist panels of First class doors, no doubt to assist in rapid identification for First class ticket holders. Another unusual feature was the decision by the railway to move directly from oil lighting to electricity, using Stones' patent system, putting the Knotty well in advance of most other railway companies.

By 1909, the script initials were superseded on all stock by the lettering "N.S.R" in gold block characters, shaded in red, shadowed in black. A typical 6-wheeled Composite carriage was now lettered: [THIRD] 277 [FIRST] N.S.R [FIRST] (knot) [FIRST] 277 [THIRD]. The device was on the bottom panel of the central door. A different style was used for the short 4-wheeled vehicles retained on the local 'loop' services. These all featured a central device, but one version had "N.S.R" above, number to the left and knot to the right; another version had the knot above the device, "N.S.R" to the left and number to the right.

It seems that during the First World War, the use of gilt transfers for the ordinary lettering was discontinued, and yellow hand-

North Staffordshire 'E' Class 0-6-0 No. 104, built by the Vulcan Foundry in 1872, as rebuilt with larger boiler in 1903, giving a nice sharp image of the Adams livery. On the original print, the black edging can just be made out, a rare occurrence.
Author's collection

North Staffordshire Railway

The first of this wheel arrangement on the NSR, 'G' Class 4-4-0 No. 86, was built in June 1910. There are several errors in this painting, but the colour is good, and the device is correctly shown on the driving wheel splasher.
Author's collection

painted characters replaced them. Yellow lining was also substituted for gold. Photographs in the Carriage Shop in 1921 seem to confirm that after the War the gilt transfers shaded in red were reinstated. It has been suggested that carriage roofs were now grey, but the photographs refute this and show that the paint shop was still painting roofs and wheel tyres white.

Non-passenger stock was originally brown, lettered "N.S.R [knot] (number)" in yellow, shaded to right and below in blue. In common with the general passenger stock from 1903, it was painted madder lake. No further details are recorded.

Wagons were always dark red brown, probably brown oxide, with ironwork on the body and below the solebar painted black. At first lettering was 6 inches high with "N.S.R" to the left. Treatment varied on open wagons and vans. Opens had a central 'knot' and the number to the right. Load was painted in italic script on the lowest plank, for example "*To Carry 6 Tons*". The number was painted on the solebar left of centre, and tare at extreme left.

Covered vans had the "N.S.R" at top left, the 'knot' at top right. The number was painted to the lower left, with load and any other special instructions to lower right. Solebar painting was the same as on the open wagons.

Cattle wagons had the lettering along the upper part of the side, no doubt to avoid being obscured by the standard limewash method of disinfectant then in use. "N.S.R" was placed to the left of the doors, with "*To Carry 8 Tons*" in script lettering on the right. On the left leaf of the doors was the number, with the knot on the right leaf. Tare and the number were on the solebar in the standard positions.

Brake vans usually featured a lot of outside framing, an upper area of flat panelling with one or two windows, and a verandah at one end only. The earliest lettering known has "N.S.R" to the left of the main part of the body and the knot to the right. Above, on the panelled area was "BREAK [window] (number)". The number also appeared centrally near the bottom of the side. This spelling of the word 'brake' was quite normal in the 19th century. Vans with two windows in the upper area had "BREAK [window] (number) [window] VAN" to accommodate this. After about 1900 it became usual to use the word 'BRAKE', but there were no other alterations.

From 1912, larger 14-inch letters were adopted for wagons, with a new cast numberplate, and it seems that from this time solebars and headstocks were painted black. Open wagons were lettered "N [knot] S", with the knot on the central drop-door. The only number was now on the solebar numberplate, which was rectangular, with "N.S.R" over the number. Tare was painted to the left of the solebar. Vans also had the large initials on each side of the doors "N [doors] S", but the knot was displaced to the lower right, with the number in a corresponding position on the lower left.

Brake vans seem to have had little alteration from the earlier period, except that the number no longer appeared on the body, just on the solebar numberplate.

Wagon sheets are reported (in 1896) to have been lettered "N.S.R", with the number, and featured a Staffordshire knot.

296
North Staffordshire Railway

The later NSR wagon lettering.

| 1 | 'Vermilion'
Carter 36
Pantone 485C
BS 5252 04 E 53
'Poppy Red' | 2 | 'Madder Lake'
Carter 31
Pantone 1815C
BS 381C 473
'Gulf Red' |

Stratford-upon-Avon & Midland Junction Railway

This small but fascinating railway was for a large proportion of its existence known as the East & West Junction Railway, opened in 1871 and 1873, although from 1877 to 1885 no passenger trains were run. Its western extremity was Stratford-upon-Avon and in the east the E&WJR joined the Northampton & Banbury Junction Railway near Towcester. The N&BJR had been opened in two stages in 1866 and 1872, and was worked by the London & North Western Railway from 1875, but the E&WJR had running powers northwards into Blisworth on the L&NWR main line. The E&WJR was extended further west from Stratford-upon-Avon to Broom Junction on the Midland Railway's Evesham and Redditch loop line in 1879 by the nominally independent Evesham, Redditch & Stratford-upon-Avon Junction Railway.

After the railway's passenger service was revived in 1885, the E&WJR was extended further east from Towcester to a junction on the Bedford to Northampton branch of the MR by the Stratford-upon-Avon, Towcester & Midland Junction Railway in 1891. The E&WJR had running powers on the Midland line as far as Olney, about 10 miles from Bedford, but apart from a short initial period the ST&MJR was used only for goods with an occasional special passenger train.

A connection to the Great Central Railway's London extension in 1899 significantly increased the status of the E&WJR. The railway, with a route mileage of fifty-two, was actually operated by a joint committee of the E&WJR and the ST&MJR. However, by an Act of 1908, the situation was simplified by creating the Stratford-upon-Avon & Midland Junction Railway from 1st January 1909 (the formal title of the S&MJR always used "upon"). The Northampton & Banbury Junction Railway was then absorbed and worked by the S&MJR in 1910, increasing the route to 67½ miles. Owing to its association with Stratford, the S&MJR styled itself 'The Shakespeare Route' in advertising.

The E&WJR, and later the S&MJR, had a small locomotive works at Stratford-upon-Avon. The Engineer of the E&WJR was Mr J.F. Burke, with Mr J. Bradshaw as Works Manager, but from 1909 the S&MJR Engineer was Mr Russell Willmot (son of the Chairman Mr Harry Willmott). In 1911 he moved to the Isle of Wight Central Railway, but was kept on in a consultative capacity. The shops at Stratford carried out day-to-day running repairs, and occasionally some heavy engineering and rebuilding. The locomotives were ordered almost entirely from Beyer, Peacock & Co. of Manchester, and heavy repairs were usually undertaken by them or other outside contractors.

The S&MJR was absorbed into the London Midland & Scottish Railway in 1923, and passed into the London Midland Region of British Railways in 1948.

The liveries of the S&MJR and its antecedents are still a matter of research, and it is only possible to present what is currently thought to be true. However, since the original article appeared (July 1998), the excellent two-volume work *The Stratford-upon-Avon & Midland Junction Railway* by Barry Taylor (Lightmoor, 2017/2018) has advanced our knowledge considerably. For brevity, the locomotives and rolling stock in use before the reopening in 1885 will be omitted.

The E&WJR by 1885 owned seven engines: one 0-6-0ST (No. 1), three outside-framed 0-6-0s (numbered 2, 3 and 4) and two 2-4-0Ts (numbered 5 and 6) all by Beyer, Peacock, plus another un-numbered engine which was an 0-6-0ST by Manning, Wardle. It seems that these locomotives were painted 'crimson lake', also described as 'lake' and 'chocolate'. These terms can be shown by many examples during the Victorian era to be synonymous with dark crimsons, and the livery was probably not dissimilar from that of the Midland Railway (see above), especially since the engines were lined out in black and yellow. Domes were polished brass, and bufferbeams were plain vermilion. Numbering was by a small cut-out brass numeral on the cab side-sheets, or on the bunkers of the 2-4-0Ts above the Beyer, Peacock maker's plate. There were no bufferbeam numbers or any indicator of ownership.

Three ex-L&NWR 'DX' Class 0-6-0s were purchased in 1891 (numbered 7, 8 and 9), which seem to have acted as a catalyst for change. The 'new' ex-L&NWR engines received proper plates and it is from this time that signs of company ownership at last begin to appear. The cast plates were small and rectangular, with incurved corners, and are thought to have been brass on a black background. Tenders or tanks carried plates lettered "E&W", having a smaller ampersand, with a similar plate carrying the number on the cabside. The plate on the tenders of the 'DX' 0-6-0s had to be off-centre to avoid a vertical line of rivet-heads.

The ex-L&NWR engines arrived in black (including, of course, their domes) and it is my belief that over the 1891-97 period, black was adopted for almost all E&WJR engines as they went through shops, and the numberplates and company plates as detailed above began to be applied to the rest of the stock. In addition, photographs

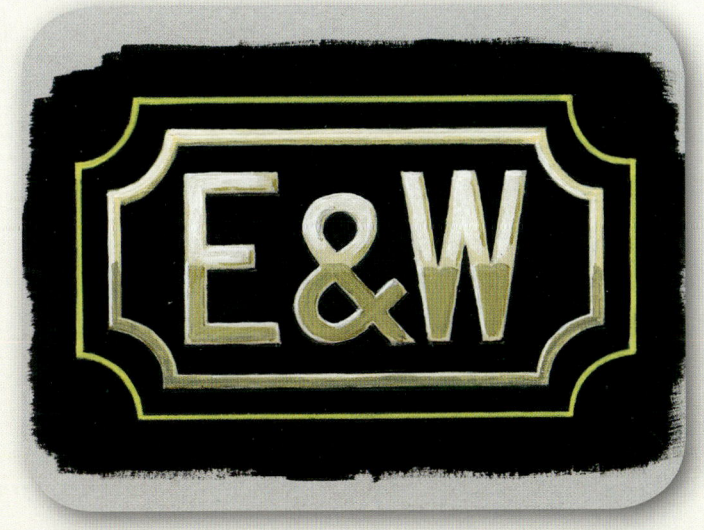

East & West Junction Railway locomotive plate and lining.

Stratford-upon-Avon & Midland Junction Railway

of the engines during this period almost certainly reveal a band of a pale colour in their lining. That this pale colour was green is confirmed by T.R. Perkins in the *Railway Magazine* of November 1902. However, Mr Perkins was several years out of date, as green had been omitted from the lining by about 1897 (see below).

The band of green lining was fine-lined on each side with yellow. Bands of the lining with incurved corners were applied to tanks and bunkers, tender sides and rear, boiler bands and sandboxes. The larger cabs of the 0-6-0s carried lining on top and bottom sidesheets, but the upper sheets of the cabs on the two tank engines had only a yellow line around the edge. Valances and outside frames were also edged with only a single yellow line.

At first, the two 2-4-0T engines, although almost certainly painted black, did not yet carry the cast plates, and their lining had rounded corners. The standard plates were applied by about 1897, the Beyer, Peacock maker's plate having to be moved to make way for the number plate. The lining was changed to have incurved corners at the same time, and was simplified to two parallel yellow lines, described below.

In 1895, No. 10 arrived, another Beyer, Peacock 0-6-0 of a very similar type to the three older Beyer, Peacock 0-6-0s. This showed that the design of numberplates was by no means finalised, as it carried both an "E&W" plate on its tender, and a cabside plate featuring "E&W" over the number. This was an isolated case and No. 10 later received a standard numberplate. The engine may also at first have been in unlined black.

There followed two more Beyer, Peacock 0-6-0s – No. 11 (1897) and No. 12 (1900). Photographs of these engines when new show unequivocally that the standard livery was black, but now lined out only in yellow. The yellow lines were quite broad in themselves, at least ⅜ inch and possibly ½ inch in width. They were applied in pairs about two inches apart to form bands on tenders, cabs, cab side-sheets, boiler bands and large sandboxes. Splashers, the inner edge of the wheel tyres and the lower edge of the outside frames had only a single yellow line. The outside cranks received a double ring of lining around the axle ends. Domes were polished brass, as were the rims of the splashers, and there was a polished brass fillet between the boiler and the smokebox. Along with the polished copper pipes and brass fittings of the injectors, and the polished steel reversing levers and coupling rods, the engines presented a very smart and sparkling appearance.

Bufferbeams had been plain vermilion during the early E&WJR period, but photographs suggest that from 1897 the engine number was applied in cut-out serif brass characters screwed to

Stratford-upon-Avon & Midland Junction Railway

the bufferbeam, e.g. "Nº [hook] 12". Most of the engines now also received lining around the edge and ends of the bufferbeam, probably in black and yellow. Buffer casings were black.

The arrival from Beyer, Peacock in 1903 of the 2-4-0 tender engine No. 13 ushers in a period of confusion for the unfortunate researcher. It has been stated in one source that No. 13, and indeed all five engines built by Beyer, Peacock in 1903-08 were painted 'dark blue', lined in black and yellow. The origin of this reference remains unclear.

Frankly, I think it is extremely unlikely. Blue may at least have been possible for No. 13, considering that it was the premier passenger engine of the line, but the remaining Beyer, Peacock engines were humble 0-6-0s, and Mr Willmott later makes no mention of any colour other than black in his interviews with the railway press. There is no support from photographs either; even dark blue appears greyish in the blue-sensitive orthochromatic emulsions of the period. In my opinion all the engines were finished in black, and it is on that basis that I will proceed.

Another 0-6-0, No. 14, arrived from Beyer, Peacock in 1903, followed by 0-6-0s No. 15 in 1904 and No. 16 in 1906. All were virtually identical, having outside frames, but differing from the earlier engines by having Belpaire fireboxes, smaller wheels and a straight top to the frames. The five engines, including 2-4-0 No. 13, were painted black with polished brass domes, and were lined out with double yellow lines in the same manner as detailed above. They also had the standard plates and brass bufferbeam numbers.

There were a number of alterations to the locomotive stock at the end of the E&WJR period. Several of the older engines were rebuilt, and two of the ex-L&NWR 'DX' Class 0-6-0s were withdrawn, leaving only No. 7 rebuilt with a new boiler in 1903. Both of the 2-4-0Ts were rebuilt with new boilers in 1907, losing their brass domes and being finished in the standard E&WJR livery of black lined with yellow, all panels having incurved corners.

By the time of the amalgamation into the S&MJR, the locomotive fleet had achieved virtual standardisation in livery, with one exception. The last locomotive in the old livery may well have been Manning, Wardle 0-6-0ST No. 1, which was described in the *Locomotive Magazine* (February 1907) as being painted 'chocolate', with the initials painted on the tank. Contemporary photographs reveal the lettering to be "E&W", with the ampersand as usual being smaller than the initials. The engine appears to have been the one that hauled the first train in 1871, but which remained un-numbered until first the Beyer, Peacock 0-6-0ST No. 1 had been sold in 1888, and its successor, Yorkshire Engine Company 2-4-0T

Stratford-upon-Avon & Midland Junction Railway

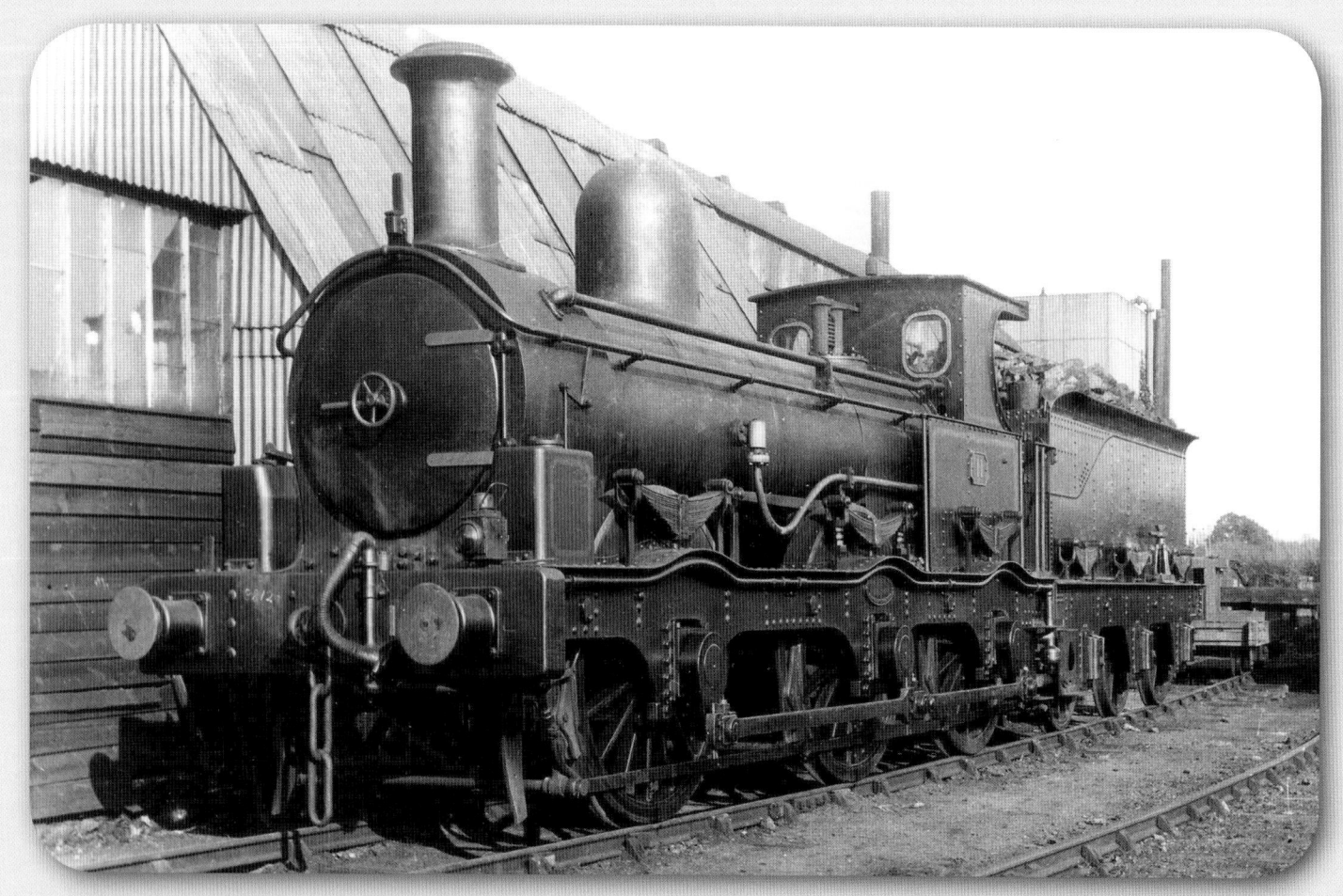

Beyer, Peacock 0-6-0 No. 11 of 1897 at Stratford circa 1924, carrying the late S&MJR livery with green lining. The Beyer, Peacock works number has been chalked onto the bufferbeam, possibly for LM&SR staff to work out their renumbering scheme. One numeral of the brass bufferbeam number can be seen.
Real Photographs

No. 1 *Hope* had been sold in 1895. The Manning, Wardle was sold in turn to the Shropshire & Montgomeryshire Light Railway in 1911.

In December 1908 there arrived from Beyer, Peacock the last new engines the line ever received, two outside-framed 0-6-0s numbered 17 and 18. Although carrying otherwise standard E&WJR livery, they were in fact lettered "SMJ" on the tenders, as described below.

After the formation of the Stratford-upon-Avon & Midland Junction Railway, several changes by Mr Willmott made themselves felt. While retaining the former E&WJR style of numberplates, the "E&W" plates were removed and "SMJ" in gold closely-spaced sans-serif letters became the standard, the transfers apparently shaded in green and white. On the bufferbeam, the "Nº" prefix was removed, leaving only the number on the right-hand side of the drawhook. Domes and other brass items formerly polished were now painted over. In 1908 some of the oldest surviving engines were put on a duplicate list, and their numbers were prefixed with a cypher, namely locomotives 01, 02, 03 and 07.

Another more important change came about, and that was the reintroduction of the green lining band. When this happened is not known, but I would suggest that it was about 1916, as 0-6-0 No. 10 was rebuilt during that year and appears to have had it applied at the time. The change was not mentioned in the railway press until 1920 (*Railway Magazine*) and 1921 (*Locomotive Magazine*), but long delays between the appearance of a change and its reporting were not uncommon. The yellow lining on each side of the green was reduced in width to a ¼ inch or less and is harder to see in photographs. At the same time, the company lettering changed to a larger style. The characters were still sans-serif, but the shading was simplified, with the white highlighting used in the earlier period much reduced.

Finally, about 1920, very small cut-out brass class letters were affixed beside the bufferbeam numbers. Class 'D' consisted of the two largest 0-6-0s, No. 17 and No. 18; Class 'C' was the 2-4-0 No. 13 and the 2-4-0Ts No. 5 and No. 6; the 0-6-0s numbered 02, 14, 15 and 16 were Class 'B'; and the remaining 0-6-0s, numbered 03, 4, 07, 11 and 12, were Class 'A'. The latter sometimes led to the erroneous assumption that the engines had been renumbered.

The locomotive list was altered in this period by the sale of the two 2-4-0Ts to the Railway Operating Division of the War Department in 1916, which was the reason that 0-6-0 No. 10 was 'resurrected' after having been withdrawn in 1914, and the withdrawal of the ex-L&NWR 0-6-0 No. 07 in 1920, to be replaced by an ex-London Brighton & South Coast engine. Ex-LB&SCR 0-6-0 No. 428 arrived at Stratford-upon-Avon in November 1920, apparently in LB&SCR goods black. The cabside number and "LBSC" on the

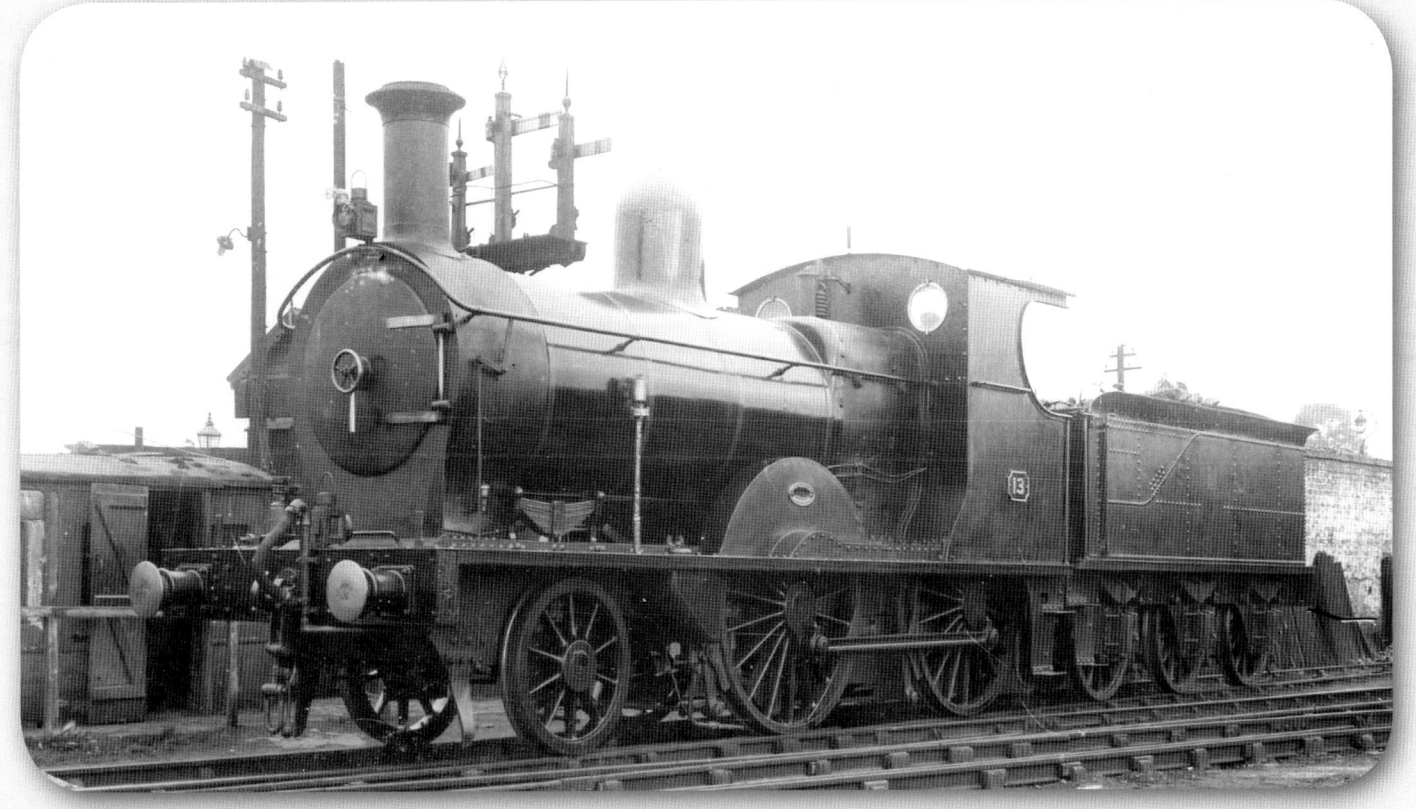

301
Stratford-upon-Avon & Midland Junction Railway

Beyer, Peacock 2-4-0 No. 13 of 1903 at Stratford in September 1922, in the late livery with green lining and larger "SMJ" on the tender. This engine was withdrawn two years later without receiving an LM&SR number. *Author's collection*

The later Beyer, Peacock 0-6-0s had straight tops to their outside frames. No. 15 of 1904 is seen at Stratford circa 1922 in the late livery. Behind the brake hose can just be detected parts of the brass bufferbeam number and the 'B' class suffix. *Real Photographs*

Stratford-upon-Avon & Midland Junction Railway

tender were painted out and the large SMJ initials and a standard numberplate applied. The engine was later repainted in the standard late livery incorporating green lining.

The most modern carriages owned by the E&WJR dated from 1885 and were 4-wheeled; four Composites, four Thirds and three Brake Thirds. When first received from the Birmingham Railway Carriage & Wagon Co., they appear to have been in a simple varnished wood finish, or possibly 'teak colour', reported in a contemporary newspaper as 'light brown'. This state of affairs was at best temporary as the livery of the E&WJR is soon reported as being 'lake' or 'chocolate' (almost certainly the same crimson colour as the original locomotives), with 'cream' upper panels. The term 'cream' often refers to the appearance of white under varnish.

In the 1890s, cream was used in the waist panels, upright panels and the top quarter panels. The main body colour was applied to the bottom quarter panels, carriage ends and the fascias or beading of the upper panels. Lining was reported as being yellow, apparently fine-lined with vermilion. The edges of the louvres of the door ventilators seem to have been picked out in stripes, possibly of the body colour, or perhaps of the lining. Horseboxes were painted 'lake' only and appear to have been unvarnished. All roofs were white.

Lettering was sans-serif, probably in gold shaded in black, but photographs are inconclusive. Class marking was in words, for example "THIRD", on the waist panel of the doors. The company name was confined to an oval garter positioned centrally on the bottom quarter panels, and vehicle numbers were applied in the waist panels, positioned symmetrically.

The new S&MJR immediately instituted a programme of carriage modernisation. The three Brake Thirds had been withdrawn in 1908, but all eight of the surviving 4-wheeled ex-E&WJR carriages were converted by 1910 into 6-wheeled vehicles and fitted with the vacuum brake. Carriage No. 10 was rebuilt from a 5-compartment Third into a twin saloon with central guard's compartment, and used by the Directors when required. Furthermore, in 1910 and 1912, six ex-Midland Railway carriages were purchased, three 6-wheeled vehicles and three bogie vehicles.

An article about the newly-formed S&MJR appeared in the *Railway Magazine* of April 1910 (and therefore probably submitted during 1909), illustrated by a photograph of composite No. 6. This carriage shows the bottom quarter panels, upright panels and top quarter panels being painted 'lake', leaving only the waist panels in cream. It has been lettered "SMJ" on the central waist panel, with the number within the oval garter below. Presumably the old E&WJR name on the garter was painted out. Class marking is in large numerals in the waist of each door. The characters are now

Stratford-upon-Avon & Midland Junction Railway

serif, probably in gold, and apparently shaded in red and shadowed in black. The ends of headstocks are lined, but the rest of the solebar appears featureless.

However, the published photograph of No. 6 is a red herring. The evidence suggests that this was actually a specially-prepared vehicle and is not truly representative of the policy of the railway. From 1909 a Midland-style carriage livery had been adopted; Saloon No. 10 was photographed in it soon after rebuilding in that year. The new livery was all-over crimson, apparently with fascias painted black, lined in gold and fine-lined vermilion. The lettering style on the all-crimson livery was of seriffed characters in gold, with large class numerals on the lower door panels. Garters as an indicator of ownership were abandoned.

The ex-Midland vehicles had their lettering shaded in red and white and shadowed in black, and therefore very possibly transfers applied by Derby before the carriages were dispatched. The special Saloon No. 10 may also have had this shading, but close photographs of the ex-E&WJR carriages now available for study show a plainer style, almost certainly with the gilt seriffed characters simply surrounded by a black line.

The company initials and numbers were placed in the waist panels. On carriages with four compartments, two numbers were arranged symmetrically on each side with the initials central, for example "7 [door] SMJ [door] 7", but on 5-compartment carriages the initials and numbers were on either side of the central door, for example: "SMJ [door] 19". Saloon No. 10 had no class marking and was lettered on each side of the pair of doors to the central luggage compartment "SMJ [GUARD][door] 10".

The E&WJR owned eleven horseboxes dating from 1885, 1898 and 1905. By 1908, the three oldest vehicles had been withdrawn, but the S&MJR purchased two more in 1909, making a total of ten horseboxes. They also acquired one 'hound van', which was an adaptation of a 4-wheeled brake van purchased from the Great Eastern Railway in 1909.

It is difficult to say what livery these vehicles carried, except that the hound van, which was more often than not used as an ordinary brake vehicle, was probably in passenger livery. On other railways it was usual to paint horseboxes in a similar fashion to the passenger stock livery; the E&WJR had used 'lake' or more probably the red-brown base colour for the lake. On the S&MJR, photographs suggest that the horseboxes were treated more like goods vehicles, even though they had Mansell wheels and were fitted with the automatic brake for use in passenger trains. The base colour was unvarnished; they and had the large initials "SMJ" on the top portion of the side doors, with the number on the drop-flap. If the horseboxes were red-brown, then it's possible that the lettering

Stratford-upon-Avon & Midland Junction Railway

in yellow, but if they were painted goods stock grey, then it was almost certainly in white.

The wagons of the E&WJR were painted a light grey, including solebars (even when steel), and black below. Strapping on the body may also have been black. Lettering seems to have been confined to the lower plank of open wagons, being about 7 inches high in white sans-serif characters split on either side of the central door. A maker's photograph has "E. & W.[door] J. R.", with square full stops, but views of wagons in traffic show that the first full stop was omitted. Tare was painted in about 3-inch numerals on the solebar, and the number was carried on a rectangular plate lettered "E&WJR^Y" and prefixed by "N^o".

When the S&MJR came into being, the wagon colour is said to have darkened to a medium grey. Running numbers were shown by a small rectangular numberplate lettered "SMJ" over the number. Large company initials "SMJ" were applied to all the stock. They were about 20 inches high on open wagons, spaced out on the body, the 'M' centrally on the door. Vans had 14-inch letters positioned on the upper right with the number painted in 6-inch numerals below. Cattle wagons had the initials and number painted in about 9-inch characters on the left-hand side of the vehicle, separated by the crossed outside framing, for example "SMJ [frame] 62". Brake vans had "SMJ" painted in 18-inch letters on the upper part of the side with the 'M' central and the 9-inch number below it.

There is little information about wagon sheets. The E&WJR sheets apparently carried the initials "E.&W.J.R." as used on the wagon stock, but no other distinguishing marks. The S&MJR sheets were very probably treated in a similar way.

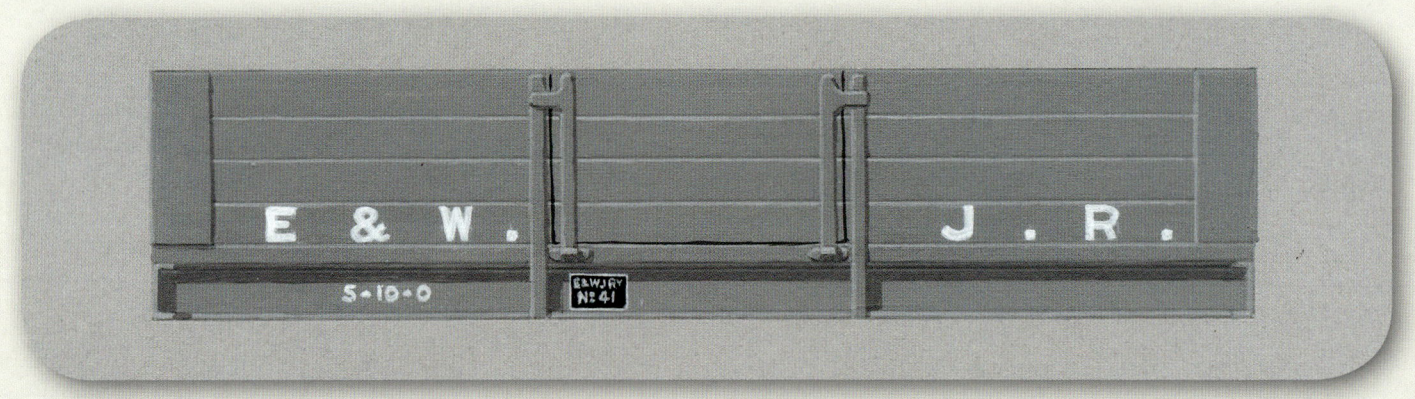

East & West Junction Railway wagon lettering.